The Muses' Library

★

THE POEMS
OF
ANDREW MARVELL

THE POEMS

OF

ANDREW MARVELL

printed from the unique copy
in the British Museum
with
some other poems
by him

edited with an introduction
by
HUGH MACDONALD

HARVARD UNIVERSITY PRESS
CAMBRIDGE, MASSACHUSETTS

First published in the Muses' Library in U.S.A.
1952 by Harvard University Press
Cambridge, Massachusetts

Second edition 1956
Reprinted 1958
Reprinted 1960

This edition first published as a paperback 1963
Reprinted 1966
Reprinted 1973

To
F. P. and Joanna
Wilson

Library of Congress Catalog Card Number 53-9848

SBN 647-67752-8

Printed in Great Britain

CONTENTS

CONTENTS

INTRODUCTION

INTRODUCTION

ANDREW MARVELL, the father of the poet, was born—so it is believed on the authority of Fuller—at Meldreth, about eight miles south of Cambridge. There is still a house called the Marvells in the village. He was educated at Emmanuel College, taking his M.A. degree in 1608. In 1610 he was a minister at Flamborough: but was inducted into the living of Winestead in Holderness on the 23rd of April 1614. He was appointed Master of the Charterhouse at Hull in 1624, in which town he was also lecturer at Holy Trinity Church. Fuller, in his *Worthies of England* (1662), describes him as 'Most *facetious* in his *discourse*, yet *grave* in his *carriage*, a most excellent preacher who like a good husband never *broached* what he had new *brewed*, but preached what he had pre-studied some competent time before... It happened that *Anno Dom.* 1640 Jan. 23 [i.e. 1641] crossing *Humber* in a *Barrow-boat*, the same was *sand-warpt*, and he drowned therein, by the *carelessness* (not to say *drunkenness*) of the boat-men, to the great grief of all good men.' In *The Rehearsall Transpros'd, the Second Part* (1673) Marvell wrote, 'But as to my Father, he dyed before ever the War broke out, having lived with some measure of reputation, both for Piety and Learning: and he was moreover a Conformist to the established Rites of the Church of *England*, although I confess none of the most over-running or eager in them.' The poet's attitude to the Church of England was probably much the same as his father's. He disliked intolerance and certainly did not belong to the school of Laud.

Andrew Marvell, the poet, was born on the 31st of March 1621 at Winestead. He was the son of his father's first wife, Anne Pease. He had three sisters older than himself; but only one, Mary, born in 1617, who married Edmond Popple in 1636, concerns us. Their son, William Popple, was educated under Marvell's guidance (*D.N.B.*) and became a London merchant and a friend of John Locke. He died in 1708. Marvell's younger brother, John, lived only for a short time.

Marvell went to Hull Grammar School, and on the 14th of December 1633 matriculated as a sizar of Trinity College, Cambridge. There is a 'life' of him prefixed to the edition of his *Works* edited by Thomas Cooke, published in 1726. This contains a story of Marvell leaving Trinity to join some Jesuits, and being found by his father in a bookseller's shop in London. But this life cannot be regarded as a very reliable authority for some of the statements it contains. Marvell contributed two sets of verses in Greek and Latin respectively to *Musa Cantabrigiensis*, published on the death of the Princess Anne in 1637. Other contributors to this collection of academical verse were Richard Crashaw and Edward King, whose death was the occasion of Milton's *Lycidas*, printed in a similar volume later in the next year. Marvell was admitted a scholar of Trinity and graduated as a B.A. in 1638. He did not become a Fellow, and left Cambridge before September 1641. He spent some years abroad, probably, as Sir Charles Firth suggests (*D.N.B.*), the years 1642 to 1646. It was during these travels that he visited Richard Flecknoe, who was in Rome from 1645 to 1647. Mr. Margoliouth has given reasons for believing that Marvell was travelling as a tutor to an Edward Skinner. The evidence is not conclusive, but that he was acting in this capacity is likely enough. He must have returned to England by 1649, as in that year he contributed verses to Lovelace's *Lucasta* and to *Lachrymæ Musarum*, published on the death of Lord

Hastings. Lord Fairfax, who had recently resigned his command, engaged Marvell as tutor to his daughter Mary in 1650 or 1651. He lived with the Fairfax family at one of their seats, Nun Appleton House in Yorkshire, till 1653, and it was during his residence there that most of his best-known poems were written. A letter from Milton to Bradshaw, recommending Marvell to the post of his assistant in the secretaryship for foreign tongues, dated 'Feb. the 21 1652 [i.e. 1653]', states that Marvell had been abroad for four years. It is in this letter that Milton uses the well-known words about Marvell as a man 'of singular desert for the State to make use of; who alsoe offers himself, if there be any employment for him'. He was not, however, selected: but he was well in with the Parliamentary leaders, and became tutor to Cromwell's ward, William Dutton. Marvell lived at Eton in the house of John Oxenbridge, a Fellow of the College. Writing to Cromwell in a letter dated 'Windsor the 28th of July 1653' Marvell gave an account of his young charge (Margoliouth, II, p. 291). In 1657 Marvell was appointed to assist Milton in the Latin Secretaryship. On the Protector's death Milton, Marvell and Dryden were allowed six yards of mourning —although the allowance to Dryden was subsequently disallowed (Legouis, p. 214). Dryden had for a time some employment under the Government.

In 1655 Marvell had published anonymously *The First Anniversary* (see p. 121). He was elected member for Hull in April 1660, and (a third time) for the Cavalier Parliament in 1661. The corporation of Hull paid Marvell and his colleague, Colonel Anthony Gilby, salaries as members for their borough. Certainly Marvell gave full service, for he kept the corporation informed of what was going on in Parliament in a series of letters, about three hundred of which are preserved among the town records of Hull. The best edition of these letters is that of Mr. Margoliouth. Marvell was active in other affairs, going to Holland in 1663 and in July of the same year joining the first Earl of Carlisle's embassy to Russia, Sweden and Denmark. He returned in January 1665. An account of the journey by Guy Miège was published in 1669, as *A Relation of Three Embassies from his Majestie Charles II to the Great Duke of Muscovy...performed by the Earl of Carlisle in the years 1663 & 1664*. He did not speak much in the Commons, although he is mentioned in *Arlington's Letters to Sir W. Temple* (1701). He made a speech upon the second reading of the Bill for securing the Protestant Religion in March 1677. For what information we have, see the 'Check-List of Persons' in *The Diary of John Milward*, edited by Caroline Robbins (1938). There can be no doubt that he was the author of the mock speech from the Throne, an amusing satire on Charles II. The text is given in most books on Marvell; it is readily available in Augustine Birrell's *Andrew Marvell* (1905) in 'The English Men of Letters' series. This mock speech was distributed in manuscript in April 1675. Earlier than this—no doubt when the fate of the Regicides was being considered—Milton's nephew, Edward Phillips, in his Life of his uncle printed in *Letters of State Written by Mr. John Milton* (1694), says that 'Mr. Andrew Marvell, a member for Hull, acted vigorously in his [Milton's] behalf and made a considerable party for him'. Milton was no doubt in some danger. That Marvell had an admiration for Milton is evident from his verses before the second edition of *Paradise Lost* (see p. 64), and his use of lines in *Lycidas*. Besides, Aubrey records that 'His [Milton's] familiar learned acquaintances were Mr. Andrew Marvell, Mr. Skinner, Dr. Pagett M.D....'

After the Restoration Marvell wrote a series of satires, the best known and longest of which is *The last Instructions to a Painter.* These pictures of t e times, whether satirical or not, had been inaugurated by Waller's *Instructions to a Painter* (1666). Under titles which varied slightly they became very popular. Some were printed, but most of those attacking the Court party, including the majority of Marvell's, were circulated in manuscript; they could have been read by comparatively few. The printing of them at the time they were written would have been too dangerous. Most of them were printed after the Revolution in *Poems on Affairs of State* first published in 1689. It has not been possible to include Marvell's political satires in this edition, although they were printed by G. A. Aitken in the original series of the Muses' Library. They have no relation to his lyrical poetry, and they contain so many allusions that they require a great deal of annotation to make them intelligible. They were an important political weapon; Marvell was probably the best-informed of the writers.

Marvell also conducted controversies in books and pamphlets. His prose writings are effective because he was both serious and amusing. In the place of the fierce attacks in several of his satires he used banter or 'drolling', as it was then called, against his adversaries. Intolerance of nonconformists was much advocated. One of the chief writers on the Church side was Samuel Parker who in 1686 became Bishop of Oxford. The case for religious toleration was expressed by Marvell, and in two books, *The Rehearsal Transpros'd* (1672) and *The Rehearsall Transpros'd, the Second Part* (1673), printed for Nathaniel Ponder, Bunyan's publisher. Marvell took up the cudgels vigorously. The *Second Part* is the more amusing. Although Marvell's disputations have little relation to his poetry, a short quotation may not be out of place: 'When he [Parker] had cook'd up these musty collections, he makes his first invitation to his *old Acquaintance* my Lord Archbishop of *Canterbury*, who had never seen before nor heard of him. But I must confess he furbishes up his Grace in so glorious an Epistle, that had not my Lord been long since proof against the most Spiritual Flattery, the Dedication only without ever reading the book might have served to have fixed him from that instant as his Favourite. Yet all this I perceive did not his work, but his Grace was so unmindful, or rather so prudent, that the Gentleman thought it necessary to spur up again the next year with another new book to show more plainly what he would be at.' Burnet wrote that 'From the king down to the trades-man his book was read with great pleasure'. Swift, who was influenced in his manner by Marvell, remarks in 'An Apology' before *A Tale of a Tub* 'we still read Marvell's Answer to Parker with Pleasure, tho' the Book it answers be sunk long ago'. In 1676 Henry Croft, Bishop of Hereford, published a pamphlet, *The Naked Truth*, which was on the side of tolerance. This was attacked by Francis Turner, Master of St. John's College, Cambridge. Marvell proceeded to ridicule Turner in *Mr. Smirke, or the Divine in Mode* (1676) in much the same way as he had ridiculed Parker. The title, *The Rehearsal Transpros'd*, was taken from Buckingham's play, *The Rehearsal*, and Mr. Smirke from the name of the parson in Etherege's *The Man of Mode*. Marvell's most important pamphlet was *An Account of the Growth of Popery in England*. This was published towards the end of 1677 and had consider-able influence on the political situation. The Govern-ment took this pamphlet seriously, but nothing hap-pened to Marvell. Stories of attempts to bribe him and to poison him exist, but the evidence for them is not strong. Marvell died about the 16th or 18th of August 1678. The exact date is uncertain (see Miss Margaret Wattie's letter to *The T.L.S.*, 2nd May 1936). He was buried in the church of St. Giles-in-the-Fields.

Marvell was a patriotic man of moderate opinions who took a somewhat detached view of events except when he considered there were serious abuses to be redressed. His attacks were directed against certain ministers of state. His opinion of Charles II seems to have been more humorous than angry. He was too independent to have been a violent partisan.

Aubrey's description of him is worth quoting in full. 'He was a great master of the Latin tongue; an excellent poet in Latin or English: for Latin verses there was no man could come into competition with him. The verses called *The Advice to a Painter* were of his making. His native towne of Hull loved him so well that they elected him for their representative in Parliament, and gave him an honourable pension to maintaine him. He was of middling stature, pretty strong sett, roundish face, cherry cheek't, hazel eie, browne haire. He was in conversation very modest, and of very few words: and though he loved wine he would never drinke hard in company, and was wont to say that *he would not play the good-fellow in any man's company in whose hands he would not trust his life*. He kept bottles of wine at his lodgeing, and many times he would drinke liberally to refresh his spirits, and exalt his muse.'

If the reader will turn to page one he will find an address 'To the Reader' signed Mary Marvell who professes to be the poet's widow. This address has puzzled people till lately, as no evidence of Marvell having ever been married has been found. Who was Mary Marvell? Cooke says in his 'Life', 'These [poems] were published with no other but a mercenary view, by a woman with whom he lodged, who hoped by this stratagem to share in what he left behind him. He was never marryed.' In a letter to *The T.L.S.* on the 14th of May 1938 Professor C. E. Ward of Duke University called attention to a Chancery suit (P.R.O. C8/252/9) from which it appeared that Mary Marvell was a servant in the house in which Marvell died. The matter was fully investigated by Professor F. S. Tupper (*P.M.L.A.*, June 1938). In June 1677 Marvell was hiding two undischarged bankrupts and holding £500 for them. He took a house in Great Russell Street in the name of Mary Palmer and there the two lay concealed. The bankrupts were Edmund Nelthorpe and Richard Thompson, both from Hull, and friends and distant connections of Marvell. The particulars are ably summarised in an Appendix to *Andrew Marvell* (1940). It was during the proceedings that Mary Palmer (alias Mary Marvell) found in Marvell's lodging in Maiden Lane, Covent Garden, 'a few books and papers of small value'. Mary Palmer claimed to be Marvell's widow, so that the money might be received by her without the Commissioners of Bankruptcy being able to seize it. The date of the address is the 15th of October 1680. As Luttrell dated his copy the 18th of January 1680/1, the book must have been on the market at the end of 1680 or early in 1681.

As Miss Bradbrook and Miss Lloyd Thomas point out, and as is, indeed, evident, the poems cannot have been much to the general taste of the time when they were published. They belong to an earlier age. It was presumably believed that an edition would sell because of Marvell's reputation in public affairs.

A few of the poems are difficult to grasp intellectually. This is not due to confusion in his own mind: he was a very lucid writer, and when he wrote the bulk of them he must have been in his fullest mental vigour. But the poems were written in private circumstances and are 'private'—or some of them are—to a peculiar degree. 'Private' poetry has always existed and is not the peculiarity of our own age. His allusions, too, are by no means always easy to trace. He was a learned man with (as has been said) a knowledge of several languages. He was very familiar with the Bible, and so far as his poems were intended to be public at all, for example, the Cromwell poems, they were addressed to those who were equally familiar with the Scriptures. There grew up legends and commentaries which expanded the texts of the classical writers and of the Bible into a mythology for which there is no full warrant in the originals. Noah's wine and its effects on him, for instance, captured the imagination of artists and writers, although his drunkenness is a small part of the Biblical account of Noah. In Marvell's day it is probable that people were much more familiar with the episode than we are now. It is less to learned commentaries of recent times that we must turn for our knowledge of how references to such events would strike a seventeenth-century reader than to, say, the sculpture or glass in cathedrals and churches.[1]

Marvell may well, too, have had in mind persons and events which are now lost to us. It is significant that the poems were not published till after his death. He lived in London and might easily, one supposes, have found a publisher had he so desired.

The first purpose of this edition is to supply a reprint of the unique copy of Marvell's *Miscellaneous Poems* of 1681.

This copy, now in the British Museum (with the shelf-mark C.59.i.8), differs from all other known copies in containing *An Horatian Ode upon Cromwell's Return from Ireland*, *The First Anniversary of the Government under O.C.* and *A Poem upon the Death of O.C.* except for the two last leaves of this last poem. The text, as I give it, has been emended in a few places. These emendations are not many, and will be found at the end of this volume. I have not given the signatures of C.59.i.8 as some appear to be misprints and so are

[1] I am indebted to Miss Helen Gardner for examples of such treatment of Biblical stories.

mere accidents. Nor have I given particulars of a second copy which contains *An Horatian Ode* and *The First Anniversary*, but not *A Poem upon the Death of O.C.* It was at one time in the possession of the late Everard Meynell, but I do not know where it is now. I have added three other poems which are not in the folio: *To . . . Mr. Richard Lovelace, Upon the Death of Lord Hastings* and *An Elegy upon the Death of My Lord Francis Villiers.* The last exists in a single exemplar in the library of Worcester College, Oxford. The authority for it being by Marvell rests on the attribution of George Clarke, an accurate scholar and a benefactor to the library; and as there is no other evidence, external or internal, to support the attribution, the verses are reprinted here for the convenience of the reader rather than from the conviction of the editor that they are by Marvell. I have omitted two early poems in Latin and Greek respectively published in the collection of academical verse at Cambridge mentioned earlier. These two poems will be found in Margoliouth's edition of Marvell's *Poems & Letters* (2 vols., The Clarendon Press, 1927).

Apart from the two copies of the folio already mentioned, all known copies collate as follows: two unsigned leaves: B–C²: D–Q⁴: R one leaf: S one leaf: T₂, T₃, T₄ (the last two unsigned): U one leaf: X one leaf. It is clear that the offending poems with flattering references to Cromwell were cancelled when the book was in the press or at least before copies could be generally distributed. It is unlikely that the last two leaves were ever printed. However, two copies did escape cancellation. C.59.i.8 collates (apart from the errors in the signatures) normally: 2 unsigned leaves: B–C²: D–U⁴. It should be added that all copies should probably contain a portrait at the beginning. I say probably as it is possible that some copies of editions of seventeenth-century books which were designed to

have a portrait may have been put on the market
without one. At any rate, neither of two fine copies
in the Bodleian which are bound up with other
folios has a portrait. The British Museum copy used
for this text was discovered by the late Bertram Dobell:
an account of it was contributed to *Notes and Queries*
for the 1st of June 1907. Besides the article itself,
information is given in Mr. Percy Dobell's *The Literature of the Restoration* (1918). The copy was bought
by G. Thorn-Drury, and later by the British Museum.
The discovery of the copy was important as until it
was found the only authority for the text and authorship of two of the Cromwell poems (as it is convenient to call them) was Captain Edward Thompson's
edition of Marvell's *Works*, which included his prose,
published in three volumes in 1776. Thompson was
genuinely interested in literature, but his critical facul-
ties were not well developed, and he included some
pieces which were recognized at once not to be Marvell's. It has been said that in a fit of disgust at the
criticism he received [1] he destroyed the manuscripts
from which he had obtained the text of two of the
Cromwell poems. Thompson's preface is, as Mr.
Margoliouth writes, a masterpiece of confusion.
Thompson seems to have had two manuscript books.
One was in part, he says, in Marvell's hand: the other
was lent to him by a descendant of William Popple,
Marvell's nephew.

More confusion, even if of a fortunate nature, has
arisen by the purchase by the Bodleian of a copy
of the folio of 1681 with manuscript corrections and
many leaves of poems in manuscript. This copy (MS.
Eng. poet. d. 49) lacks seven of the original leaves.
In the place of the cancel leaf 'S' there are eleven
leaves in manuscript containing *An Horatian Ode* and

---

[1] See *the Gentlemans Magazine for* 1776 (under Marvell in the
index).

The First Anniversary. After leaf 'X' there are seven leaves in manuscript containing *A Poem upon the Death of His Highness the Lord Protector*. These seven leaves are followed by a blank leaf, and after the blank many leaves of satires.

In the *Bodleian Library Record*, May 1945, there is a note on the purchase in which it is said that the volume 'was certainly used by Edward Thompson for his edition of Marvell's Works (1776) and may be the volume lent to Thompson by a descendant of William Popple, Marvell's nephew'. It may possibly be the one said by Thompson to have been 'written by William Popple', although Dr. R. W. Hunt is of opinion that the writing does not resemble specimens of Popple's handwriting in the Bodleian. The volume was purchased from Messrs. B. H. Blackwell, but from what source cannot now be traced. It may have been in the possession of Thomas Hollis, but this is a surmise. It is of some value textually and I have cited it here and there in my notes. At any rate it is the primary source of the last two leaves of the text of *A Poem upon the Death of Cromwell*, which, as has been said earlier, are not in B.M. C.59.i.8.

The following are the chief editions of Marvell: *The Works of Andrew Marvell* edited by Thomas Cooke, 2 vols., 1726, reprinted by T. Davies in 1772. In 1767 an edition to be edited by Bowyer & Baron was suggested by Thomas Hollis. Nothing came of this, but Hollis gave Captain E. Thompson some help in his edition of Marvell's *Works* (3 vols., 1776). Dr. Grosart published Marvell's *Works* in 1872. His edition was reprinted in 1872 and 1875. G. A. Aitken's edition of his *Poems* and *Satires* was included in the original Muses Library (2 vols., 1892). There was also an American edition published at Boston in 1857, and reprinted in England in 1881. By far the best edition of the poems, satires and letters is that by H. M. Margoliouth (2 vols.,

1927). This has already been referred to. The *D.N.B.* contains an admirable life by Sir Charles Firth in which early biographical sources are given. Augustine Birrell's *Andrew Marvell* (1905) is not only eminently readable, but is valuable because Birrell, like Marvell, was for long a member of the House of Commons. The standard book on the poet is Pierre Legouis's *André Marvell, poète, puritain, patriote, 1621–1678* (Paris and the Oxford University Press, 1928). Miss M. C. Bradbrook's and Miss M. G. Lloyd Thomas's *Andrew Marvell* (1940) contains some valuable criticism. There are several books containing criticism such as *Seven Types of Ambiguity* and *Some Versions of Pastoral* by William Empson.

I have not attempted to annotate the Latin poems: nor have I recorded the few corrections.

The portrait here reproduced is that in the National Portrait Gallery. Sir Henry Hake kindly compared this with the rough engraving in the folio. He considered that the engraving is based on this portrait. The engraving is poor and was hardly worth reproducing here. I have also to thank Mr. H. M. Margoliouth whom I have consulted on several occasions for his help. I have discussed some points with Mrs. Catherine Ing, who gave me useful advice. I am grateful to Mr. A. H. Smith, the Warden of New College, for his hospitality when I was living some distance from Oxford. Father A. Shields explained the probable meaning of geometrick year, see p. 202, l. 18.

Mrs. Duncan Jones calls my attention to her letter to the *T.L.S.*, 2nd December 1949, in which she shows that Marvell was at Saumur with Dutton in August 1656. See also *T.L.S.*, 31st July 1953.

COMMENTS
AND APPRECIATIONS

COMMENTS
AND APPRECIATIONS

As has been said above, Marvell was only known by
most people as a man of affairs, and by some as a
satirist, till his folio volume appeared in 1681. Even
then his poetry probably did not catch the attention
of many readers as his 'metaphysical' way of writing
was out of date, although Cowley continued to retain
a certain popularity. Dryden, who could not have
relished the lines before the second edition of *Paradise
Lost*, and was strongly on the Court side, wrote in the
preface to *Religio Laici* (1682), 'Those [admonitions
to Parliament against the whole Government Eccle-
siastical] not succeeding, Satyre and Rayling was the
next: And *Martin-Mar-Prelate* (the *Marvel* of those
times) was the first Presbyterian Scribbler, who
sanctify'd Libels and Scurrility to the use of the
Good Old Cause.'

By 1716 a change in taste was setting in, and 'The
Garden' as well as other poems by Marvell were
included in *Miscellany Poems. The Fourth Edition*
(6 vols.), published in that year. Cooke's edition of
the works was published in 1726, and reprinted by T.
Davies in 1772. Although Marvell is not mentioned
by Dr. Johnson, except in connection with Milton, he
must have been reasonably popular during the eigh-
teenth century to have justified Thompson's edition
of 1776. But it is not till the nineteenth century that
appreciations are found. The poet, Thomas Campbell,
gives a few selections from him in his *Specimens of the
British Poets* (1819).

Hazlitt and Lamb both admired Marvell. Lamb
in 'The Old Benchers of the Inner Temple' wrote,
'It was a pretty device of the gardener, recorded by

Marvell, who, in the days of artificial gardening, made a dial out of herbs and flowers. I must quote his verses a little higher up, for they are full, as all his serious poetry was, of a witty delicacy.' Lamb goes on to quote:

> What wondrous life is this I lead.

Two allusions to Marvell's poetry will be found in Lamb's *Letters*. He was taken with Marvell's turn for the whimsical.

Admirable as Birrell's *Andrew Marvell* (1905) is, it can hardly be called a critical work. Marvell has never been given the kind of attention bestowed, for instance, on Donne: it is possible to gather only a few comments from various modern writers. In *A Short History of English Literature* (1898) George Saintsbury wrote, 'he had reached middle life, and exhibits with a form individual and in a type more chastened and classical, the best characteristics of the Cavalier poets ... But perhaps it is not fanciful to argue that the peculiar and indeed unique perfection of phrase characterising the best poetry of this period involved a kind of mental effort of gestation which could not be repeated very often, and which obliged the poet to be either unequal or else infertile.'

'But the strongest personality of all is Andrew Marvell. Apart from Milton he is the most interesting personality between Donne and Dryden, and at his very best a finer poet than either. Most of his descriptive poems lie a little outside my beat, though I have claimed *The Garden* as metaphysical

> Annihilating all that's made
> To a green thought in a green shade,

as I might have claimed *The Nymph and the Faun* had space permitted. But his few love poems and his few devotional pieces are perfect exponents of all the "metaphysical" qualities—passionate, paradoxical argument touched with humour and learned imagery... and above all the sudden soar of passion in bold and felicitous image, in clangerous lines,

> But at my back I always hear
> Time's winged chariot hurrying near [etc.]

These lines seem to me the very roof and crown of the metaphysical love lyric, at once fantastic and passionate.'

> Sir Herbert Grierson, *Metaphysical Lyrics & Poems* (1921).

'For some poems by that writer [Marvell], then with difficulty accessible, he had a special admiration: delighting to read, with a voice hardly yet to me silent, and dwelling more than once on the magnificent hyperbole, the powerful union of pathos and humour in the lines "To his coy Mistress" where Marvell there says:

> Had we but world enough, and time,
> This coyness lady were no crime...
> ...I would
> Love you ten years before the Flood:
> And you should if you please refuse
> Till the conversion of the Jews...

Youth, therefore, Marvell proceeds, is the time for love:

> Let us roll all our strength, and all
> Our sweetness up into one ball,
> And tear our pleasures with rough strife
> Through the iron gates of life:

on this line remarking that he could fancy *grates* would have intensified Marvell's image.'

> Personal Recollections by F. T.
> Palgrave from *Alfred Lord
> Tennyson, a Memoir*, vol. ii,
> 1897.

'As a poet Marvell is very unequal. He has depth of feeling, descriptive power, melody; his study of the classics could not fail to teach him form; sometimes we find in him an airy and tender grace which remind us of the lighter manner of Milton; but art with him was only an occasional recreation, not a regular pursuit: he is often slovenly, sometimes intolerably diffuse, especially when he is seduced by the facility of the octosyllabic couplet.'

> Goldwin Smith in T. H. Ward's
> *The English Poets* (1880).

'A third and final division of Marvell's lyrics would comprise his poems upon nature; and here we have Marvell at his best, because here he lets his passion inspire him. Except in Shakespeare we have little passion for nature between Chaucer and Marvell; but in Marvell the love for natural beauty is not short of passion. Of course his love is not for wild nature—a feeling which only dates from Gray and Wordsworth —but for the ordinary country scenes,

> Fragrant gardens, shady woods
> Deep meadows and transparent floods,

and for these he brings the eye of a genuine lover and, what is more, a patient observer.'

[Canon Beeching then quotes the lines on the woodpecker in 'Appleton House'.]

'In his poem called "The Garden" Marvell has sung a palinode that for richness of phrasing in its sheer

sensuous love of garden delights is perhaps un-
matchable.'

H. C. Beeching, *The National Review*, 1901.

The most sensitive criticism of Marvell's poetry is
in Mr. T. S. Eliot's essay printed in *The Times Literary
Supplement*, 31st of March 1921. It was reprinted in
Andrew Marvell ... Tercentenary Tributes (1922) to
which Bishop Hensley Henson, Sir Edmund Gosse and
others also contributed. Bishop Henson's sermon at
Hull gives an admirable picture of Marvell the man:
he quotes Wordsworth's sonnet:

Great men have been among us; hands that penned
And tongues that uttered wisdom—better none:
The later Sidney, Marvel, Harrington,
Young Vane, and others who called Milton friend.

Mr. Birrell, who also spoke, emphasized the fact that
Marvell was no bigot by quoting the poet's well-
known comment on the Civil War.

'Whether it be a war of religion or of liberty it is
not worth the labour to enquire. Whatsoever was at
the top, the other was at the bottom; but upon con-
sidering all, I think the cause was too good to have
been fought for. Men ought to have trusted God—
they ought to have trusted the King with the whole
matter.'

Mr. Eliot's essay is too subtle to make quotation
easy. A sentence must suffice.

'Jonson never wrote anything as pure as Marvell's
Horatian Ode; but this ode has that same quality of
wit which was diffused over the whole Elizabethan
product and concentrated in the work of Jonson.
And, as was said before, this wit which pervades the
poetry of Marvell is more Latin, more refined, than
anything that succeeded it.'

'But the principal clue to Marvell's nature-mysticism lies, I think, in the obsession that green had for him. Most commentators on Marvell have remarked upon his frequent use of the word, but none except M. Legouis has laid quite sufficient stress upon its significance in his vocabulary. He used it in and out of season, moreover he supplemented it by constant references to shade and shadow, which were all part of the same line of thought. Marvell was highly sensitive to colour—an argument which could be substantiated by numerous instances;—all variations of light and shade were to him a perpetual delight; but of all colours it was green that enchanted him most; the world of his mind was a glaucous world, as though he lived in a coppice, stippled with sunlight and alive with moving shadows.'

V. Sackville West, *Andrew Marvell* (1929).

'Andrew Marvell's life and achievements were of a sure and civilized kind which do not so readily invite analysis as acceptance. During three centuries he has fortified English tradition in very different ways. From the time of his death till the beginning of the nineteenth century he was remembered as a brave and powerful fighter against intolerance, both political and ecclesiastical: so Wordsworth remembered him. Throughout the nineteenth century his reputation as a poet increased, but it was that of a poet of nature and simplicity; in the introduction to his *Works* the delightfully impassioned Grosart describes him in terms which would have been more suitably applied by the Poet Laureate to the Prince Consort. In the twentieth century Marvell's reputation as a lyric poet has grown till his finest poems have been compared, to their advantage, with Donne's.'

M. C. Bradbrook and M. G. Lloyd Thomas, *Andrew Marvell* (1940).

THE POEMS

MISCELLANEOUS
POEMS.

BY
ANDREW MARVELL, Esq;

Late Member of the Honourable House of Commons.

LONDON,

Printed for *Robert Boulter*, at the *Turks-Head*
in *Cornhill*. M.DC. LXXXI.

TO
THE READER

THESE are to Certifie every Ingenious Reader, that all these Poems, as also the other things in this Book contained, are Printed according to the exact Copies of my late dear Husband, under his own Hand-Writing, being found since his Death among his other Papers, Witness my Hand this 15*th* day of *October*, 1680.

Mary Marvell

THE POEMS

A Dialogue between the Resolved Soul and Created Pleasure

COURAGE my Soul, now learn to wield
The weight of thine immortal Shield.
Close on thy Head thy Helmet bright.
Ballance thy Sword against the Fight.
See where an Army, strong as fair,   5
With silken Banners spreads the air.
Now, if thou bee'st that thing Divine,
In this day's Combat let it shine:
And shew that Nature wants an Art
To conquer one resolved Heart.   10

Pleasure

Welcome the Creations Guest,
Lord of Earth, and Heavens Heir.
Lay aside that Warlike Crest,
And of Nature's banquet share:
Where the Souls of fruits and flow'rs   15
Stand prepar'd to heighten yours.

Soul

I sup above, and cannot stay
To bait so long upon the way.

Pleasure

On these downy Pillows lye,
Whose soft Plumes will thither fly: 20
On these Roses strow'd so plain
Lest one Leaf thy Side should strain.

Soul

My gentler Rest is on a Thought,
Conscious of doing what I ought.

Pleasure

If thou bee'st with Perfumes pleas'd,   25
Such as oft the Gods appeas'd,
Thou in fragrant Clouds shalt show
Like another God below.

Soul

A Soul that knowes not to presume
Is Heaven's and its own perfume.   30

Pleasure

Every thing does seem to vie
Which should first attract thine Eye:
But since none deserves that grace,
In this Crystal view *thy* face.

Soul

When the Creator's skill is priz'd   35
The rest is all but Earth disguis'd.

Pleasure

Heark how Musick then prepares
For thy Stay these charming Aires;
Which the posting Winds recall,
And suspend the Rivers Fall.   40

Soul

Had I but any time to lose,
On this I would it all dispose.
Cease Tempter. None can chain a mind
Whom this sweet Chordage cannot bind.

4

CHORUS

Earth cannot shew so brave a Sight   **45**
As when a single Soul does fence
The Batteries of alluring Sense,
And Heaven views it with delight.
    Then persevere: for still new Charges sound:
    And if thou overcom'st thou shalt be crown'd.

Pleasure

All this fair, and soft, and sweet,   **51**
    Which scatteringly doth shine,
Shall within one Beauty meet,
    And she be only thine.

Soul

If things of Sight such Heavens be,   **55**
What Heavens are those we cannot see?

Pleasure

Where so e're thy Foot shall go
    The minted Gold shall lie;
Till thou purchase all below,
    And want new Worlds to buy.   **60**

Soul

Wer't not a price who'ld value Gold?
And that's worth nought that can be sold.

Pleasure

Wilt thou all the Glory have
    That War or Peace commend?
Half the World shall be thy Slave   **65**
    The other half thy Friend.

Soul

What Friends, if to my self untrue?
What Slaves, unless I captive you?

Pleasure

Thou shalt know each hidden Cause;
   And see the future Time: 70
Try what depth the Centre draws;
   And then to Heaven climb.

Soul

None thither mounts by the degree
Of Knowledge, but Humility.

CHORUS

Triumph, triumph, victorious Soul;   75
The World has not one Pleasure more:
The rest does lie beyond the Pole,
And is thine everlasting Store.

On a Drop of Dew

SEE how the Orient Dew,
Shed from the Bosom of the Morn
   Into the blowing Roses,
Yet careless of its Mansion new;
For the clear Region where 'twas born   5
   Round in its self incloses:
   And in its little Globes Extent,
Frames as it can its native Element.
How it the purple flow'r does slight,
   Scarce touching where it lyes,   10
   But gazing back upon the Skies,
   Shines with a mournful Light;

Like its own Tear,
Because so long divided from the Sphear.
   Restless it roules and unsecure,   **15**
      Trembling lest it grow impure:
  Till the warm Sun pitty it's Pain,
And to the Skies exhale it back again.
      So the Soul, that Drop, that Ray
Of the clear Fountain of Eternal Day,   **20**
Could it within the humane flow'r be seen,
      Remembring still its former height,
      Shuns the sweat leaves and blossoms green;
      And, recollecting its own Light,
Does, in its pure and circling thoughts, express **25**
The greater Heaven in an Heaven less.
      In how coy a Figure wound,
      Every way it turns away:
    So the World excluding round,
      Yet receiving in the Day.   **30**
      Dark beneath, but bright above:
      Here disdaining, there in Love.
  How loose and easie hence to go:
  How girt and ready to ascend.
    Moving but on a point below,   **35**
  It all about does upwards bend.
Such did the Manna's sacred Dew destil;
White, and intire, though congeal'd and chill.
Congeal'd on Earth: but does, dissolving, run
Into the Glories of th' Almighty Sun.   **40**

Ros

CERNIS ut *Eoi* descendat Gemmula Roris,
  Inque Rosas roseo transfluat orta sinu.
Sollicitâ Flores stant ambitione supini,
  Et certant foliis pellicuisse suis.

Illa tamen patriae lustrans fastigia Sphærae,   5
   Negligit hospitii limina picta novi.
Inque sui nitido conclusa voluminis orbe,
   Exprimit ætherei quâ licet Orbis aquas.
En ut odoratum spernat generosior *Ostrum*,
   Vixque premat casto mollia strata pede.   10
Suspicit at longis distantem obtutibus Axem,
   Inde & languenti lumine pendet amans,
Tristis, & in liquidum mutata dolore dolorem,
   Marcet, uti roseis Lachryma fusa Genis.
Ut pavet, & motum tremit irrequieta Cubile,   15
   Et quoties *Zephyro* fluctuat Aura, fugit.
Qualis inexpertam subeat formido Puellam,
   Sicubi nocte redit incomitata domum.
Sic & in horridulas agitatur Gutta procellas,
   Dum prae virgineo cuncta pudore timet.   20
Donec oberrantem Radio clemente vaporet,
   Inque jubar reducem Sol genitale trahat.
Talis, in humano si possit flore videri,
   Exul ubi longas Mens agit usque moras;
Haec quoque natalis meditans convivia Cœli,   25
   Evertit Calices, purpureosque Thoros.
Fontis stilla sacri, Lucis scintilla perennis,
   Non capitur *Tyriâ* veste, vapore *Sabae*.
Tota sed in proprii secedens luminis Arcem,
   Colligit in Gyros se sinuosa breves.   30
Magnorumque sequens Animo convexa Deorum,
   Sydereum parvo fingit in Orbe Globum.
Quam bene in aversae modulum contracta figurae
   Oppositum Mundo claudit ubique latus.
Sed bibit in speculum radios ornata rotundum; 35
   Et circumfuso splendet aperta Die.
Qua Superos spectat rutilans, obscurior infra;
   Caetera dedignans, ardet amore Poli.
Subsilit, hinc agili Poscens discedere motu,
   Undique coelesti cincta soluta Viæ.   40
Totaque in aereos extenditur orbita cursus;

Hinc punctim carpens, mobile stringit iter.
Haud aliter Mensis exundans Manna beatis
    Deserto jacuit Stilla gelata solo:
Stilla gelata solo, sed Solibus hausta benignis,   **45**
    Ad sua quâ cecidit purior Astra redit.

The Coronet

WHEN for the Thorns with which I long, too long,
    With many a piercing wound,
    My Saviours head have crown'd,
I seek with Garlands to redress that Wrong:
    Through every Garden, every Mead,   **5**
I gather flow'rs (my fruits are only flow'rs)
    Dismantling all the fragrant Towers
That once adorned my Shepherdesses head.
And now when I have summ'd up all my store,
    Thinking (so I my self deceive)   **10**
    So rich a Chaplet thence to weave
As never yet the king of Glory wore:
    Alas I find the Serpent old
    That, twining in his speckled breast,
    About the flow'rs disguis'd does fold,   **15**
    With wreaths of Fame and Interest.
Ah, foolish Man, that would'st debase with them
And mortal Glory, Heaven's Diadem!
But thou who only could'st the Serpent tame,
Either his slipp'ry knots at once untie,   **20**
And disintangle all his winding Snare:
Or shatter too with him my curious frame:
And let these wither, so that he may die,
Though set with Skill and chosen out with Care.   **24**
That they, while Thou on both their Spoils dost tread,
May crown thy Feet, that could not crown thy Head.

Eyes and Tears

I

How wisely Nature did decree,
With the same Eyes to weep and see!
That, having view'd the object vain,
They might be ready to complain.

II

And, since the Self-deluding Sight,   5
In a false Angle takes each hight;
These Tears which better measure all,
Like wat'ry Lines and Plummets fall.

III

Two Tears, which Sorrow long did weigh
Within the Scales of either Eye,   10
And then paid out in equal Poise,
Are the true price of all my Joyes.

IV

What in the World most fair appears,
Yea even Laughter, turns to Tears:
And all the Jewels which we prize,   15
Melt in these Pendants of the Eyes.

V

I have through every Garden been,
Amongst the Red, the White, the Green;
And yet, from all the flow'rs I saw,
No Hony, but these Tears could draw.   20

VI

So the all-seeing Sun each day
Distills the World with Chymick Ray;
But finds the Essence only Showers,
Which straight in pity back he powers.

VII

Yet happy they whom Grief doth bless,   25
That weep the more, and see the less:
And, to preserve their Sight more true,
Bath still their Eyes in their own Dew.

VIII

*So *Magdalen*, in Tears more wise
Dissolv'd those captivating Eyes,   30
Whose liquid Chaines could flowing meet
To fetter her Redeemers feet.

IX

Not full sailes hasting loaden home,
Nor the chast Ladies pregnant Womb,
Nor *Cynthia* Teeming show's so fair,   35
As two Eyes swoln with weeping are.

X

The sparkling Glance that shoots Desire,
Drench'd in these Waves, does lose its fire.
Yea oft the Thund'rer pitty takes
And here the hissing Lightning slakes.   40

XI

The Incense was to Heaven dear,
Not as a Perfume, but a Tear.
And Stars shew lovely in the Night,
But as they seem the Tears of Light.

XII

Ope then mine Eyes your double Sluice,   **45**
And practise so your noblest Use.
For others too can see, or sleep;
But only humane Eyes can weep.

XIII

Now like two Clouds dissolving, drop,
And at each Tear in distance stop: 50
Now like two Fountains trickle down:
Now like two floods o'return and drown.

XIIII

Thus let your Streams o'reflow your Springs,
Till Eyes and Tears be the same things:
And each the other's difference bears;   55
These weeping Eyes, those seeing Tears.

*Magdala, *lascivos sic quum dimisit Amantes,*
   Fervidaque in castas lumina solvit aquas;
Hæsit in irriguo lachrymarum compede Christus,
   Et tenuit sacros uda Catena pedes.   60

Bermudas

WHERE the remote *Bermudas* ride
In th' Oceans bosome unespy'd,
From a small Boat, that row'd along,
The listning Winds receiv'd this Song.
   What should we do but sing his Praise   5
That led us through the watry Maze,
Unto an Isle so long unknown,
And yet far kinder than our own?
Where he the huge Sea-Monsters wracks,

That lift the Deep upon their Backs.   10
He lands us on a grassy Stage;
Safe from the Storms, and Prelat's rage.
He gave us this eternal Spring,
Which here enamells every thing;
And sends the Fowl's to us in care,   15
On daily Visits through the Air.
He hangs in shades the Orange bright,
Like golden Lamps in a green Night.
And does in the Pomgranates close,
Jewels more rich than *Ormus* show's.   20
He makes the Figs our mouths to meet;
And throws the Melons at our feet.
But Apples plants of such a price,
No Tree could ever bear them twice.
With Cedars, chosen by his hand,   25
From *Lebanon*, he stores the Land.
And makes the hollow Seas, that roar,
Proclaime the Ambergris on shoar.
He cast (of which we rather boast)
The Gospels Pearl upon our Coast.   30
And in these Rocks for us did frame
A Temple, where to sound his Name.
Oh let our Voice his Praise exalt,
Till it arrive at Heavens Vault:
Which thence (perhaps) rebounding, may   35
Eccho beyond the *Mexique Bay*.
Thus sung they, in the *English* boat,
An holy and a chearful Note,
And all the way, to guide their Chime,
With falling Oars they kept the time.   40

Clorinda and Damon

C. DAMON come drive thy flocks this way.
D. No: 'tis too late they went astray.
C. I have a grassy Scutcheon spy'd,
    Where *Flora* blazons all her pride.
    The Grass I aim to feast thy Sheep: **5**
    The Flow'rs I for thy Temples keep.
D. Grass withers; and the Flow'rs too fade.
C. Seize the short Joyes then, ere they vade.
    Seest thou that unfrequented Cave?
D. That den? *C.* Loves Shrine. *D.* But Virtue's
    Grave.   **10**
C. In whose cool bosome we may lye
    Safe from the Sun. *D.* not Heaven's Eye.
C. Near this, a Fountaines liquid Bell
    Tinkles within the concave Shell.
D. Might a Soul bath there and be clean,   **15**
    Or slake its Drought? *C.* What is't you mean?
D. These once had been enticing things,
    Clorinda, Pastures, Caves, and Springs.
C. And what late change? *D.* The other day
    Pan met me. *C.* What did great *Pan* say?   **20**
D. Words that transcend poor Shepherds skill,
    But He ere since my Songs does fill:
    And his Name swells my slender Oate.
C. Sweet must *Pan* sound in *Damons* Note.
D. *Clorinda's* voice might make it sweet.   **25**
C. Who would not in *Pan's* Praises meet?

CHORUS

Of Pan *the flowry Pastures sing,*
Caves eccho, and the Fountains ring.
Sing then while he doth us inspire;
For all the World is our Pan's *Quire.*   **30**

14

A Dialogue between the Soul and Body

Soul

O WHO shall, from this Dungeon, raise
A Soul inslav'd so many wayes?
With bolts of Bones, that fetter'd stands
In Feet; and manacled in Hands.
Here blinded with an Eye; and there   5
Deaf with the drumming of an Ear.
A Soul hung up, as 'twere, in Chains
Of Nerves, and Arteries, and Veins.
Tortur'd, besides each other part,
In a vain Head, and double Heart.   10

Body

O who shall me deliver whole,
From bonds of this Tyrannic Soul?
Which, stretcht upright, impales me so,
That mine own Precipice I go;
And warms and moves this needless Frame: 15
(A fever could but do the same.)
And, wanting where its spight to try,
Has made me live to let me dye.
A Body that could never rest,
Since this ill Spirit it possest.   20

Soul

What Magick could me thus confine
Within anothers Grief to pine?
Where whatsoever it complain,
I feel, that cannot feel, the pain.
And all my Care its self employes,   25
That to preserve, which me destroys:
Constrain'd not only to indure
Diseases, but, whats worse, the Cure:

And ready oft the Port to gain,
Am Shipwrackt into Health again.   30

Body

But Physick yet could never reach
The Maladies Thou me dost teach;
Whom first the Cramp of Hope does Tear:
And then the Palsie Shakes of Fear.
The Pestilence of Love does heat: 35
Or Hatred's hidden Ulcer eat.
Joy's chearful Madness does perplex:
Or Sorrow's other Madness vex.
Which Knowledge forces me to know;
And Memory will not foregoe.   40
What but a Soul could have the wit
To build me up for Sin so fit?
So Architects do square and hew,
Green Trees that in the Forest grew.

The Nymph complaining for
the death of her Faun

THE wanton Troopers riding by
Have shot my Faun and it will dye.
Ungentle men! They cannot thrive
To kill thee. Thou neer didst alive
Them any harm: alas nor cou'd   5
Thy death yet do them any good.
I'me sure I never wisht them ill;
Nor do I for all this; nor will:
But, if my simple Pray'rs may yet
Prevail with Heaven to forget   10
Thy murder, I will Joyn my Tears
Rather then fail. But, O my fears!

16

It cannot dye so. Heavens King
Keeps register of every thing:
And nothing may we use in vain.   15
Ev'n Beasts must be with justice slain;
Else Men are made their *Deodands*.
Though they should wash their guilty hands
In this warm life blood, which doth part
From thine, and wound me to the Heart,   20
Yet could they not be clean: their Stain
Is dy'd in such a Purple Grain.
There is not such another in
The World, to offer for their Sin.

    Unconstant *Sylvio*, when yet   25
I had not found him counterfeit,
One morning (I remember well)
Ty'd in this silver Chain and Bell,
Gave it to me: nay and I know
What he said then; I'me sure I do.   30
Said He, look how your Huntsman here
Hath taught a Faun to hunt his *Dear*.
But *Sylvio* soon had me beguil'd.
This waxed tame; while he grew wild,
And quite regardless of my Smart,   35
Left me his Faun, but took his Heart.

    Thenceforth I set my self to play
My solitary time away,
With this: and very well content,
Could so mine idle Life have spent   40
For it was full of sport; and light
Of foot, and heart; and did invite,
Me to its game: it seem'd to bless
Its self in me. How could I less
Than love it? O I cannot be   45
Unkind, t' a Beast that loveth me.

    Had it liv'd long, I do not know
Whether it too might have done so

17

As *Sylvio* did: his Gifts might be
Perhaps as false or more than he. 50
But I am sure, for ought that I
Could in so short a time espie,
Thy Love was far more better then
The love of false and cruel men.

   With sweetest milk, and sugar, first 55
I it at mine own fingers nurst.
And as it grew, so every day
It wax'd more white and sweet than they.
It had so sweet a Breath! And oft
I blusht to see its foot more soft, 60
And white, (shall I say then my hand?)
NAY any Ladies of the Land.

   It is a wond'rous thing, how fleet
'Twas on those little silver feet.
With what a pretty skipping grace, 65
It oft would challenge me the Race:
And when 'thad left me far away,
'Twould stay, and run again, and stay.
For it was nimbler much than Hindes;
And trod, as on the four Winds. 70

   I have a Garden of my own,
But so with Roses over grown,
And Lillies, that you would it guess
To be a little Wilderness.
And all the Spring time of the year 75
It onely loved to be there.
Among the beds of Lillyes, I
Have sought it oft, where it should lye;
Yet could not, till it self would rise,
Find it, although before mine Eyes. 80
For, in the flaxen Lillies shade,
It like a bank of Lillies laid.
Upon the Roses it would feed,
Until its Lips ev'n seem'd to bleed:
And then to me 'twould boldly trip, 85

And print those Roses on my Lip.
But all its chief delight was still
On Roses thus its self to fill:
And its pure virgin Limbs to fold
In whitest sheets of Lillies cold.   90
Had it liv'd long, it would have been
Lillies without, Roses within.
   O help! O help! I see it faint:
And dye as calmely as a Saint.
See how it weeps. The Tears do come   95
Sad, slowly dropping like a Gumme.
So weeps the wounded Balsome: so
The holy Frankincense doth flow.
The brotherless *Heliades*
Melt in such Amber Tears as these.   100
   I in a golden Vial will
Keep these two crystal Tears; and fill
It till it do o'reflow with mine;
Then place it in *Diana's* Shrine.
   Now my sweet Faun is vanish'd to   105
Whether the Swans and Turtles go:
In fair *Elizium* to endure,
With milk-white Lambs, and Ermins pure.
O do not run too fast: for I
Will but bespeak they Grave, and dye.   110
   First my unhappy Statue shall
Be cut in Marble; and withal,
Let it be weeping too: but there
Th' Engraver sure his Art may spare;
For I so truly thee bemoane,   115
That I shall weep though I be Stone:
Until my Tears, still dropping, wear
My breast, themselves engraving there.
There at my feet shalt thou be laid,
Of purest Alabaster made: 120
For I would have thine Image be
White as I can, though not as Thee.

Young Love

I

COME little Infant, Love me now,
    While thine unsuspected years
Clear thine aged Fathers brow
    From cold Jealousie and Fears.

II

Pretty surely 'twere to see   5
    By young Love old Time beguil'd:
While our Sportings are as free
    As the Nurses with the Child.

III

Common beauties stay fifteen;
    Such as yours should swifter move;   10
Whose fair Blossoms are too green
    Yet for Lust, but not for Love.

IV

Love as much the snowy Lamb
    Or the wanton Kid does prize,
As the lusty Bull or Ram,   15
    For his morning Sacrifice.

V

Now then love me: time may take
    Thee before thy time away:
Of this Need wee'l Virtue make,
    And learn Love before we may.   20

VI

So we win of doubtful Fate;
  And, if good she to us meant,
We that Good shall antedate,
  Or, if ill, that Ill prevent.

VII

Thus as Kingdomes, frustrating   **25**
  Other Titles to their Crown,
In the craddle crown their King,
  So all Forraign Claims to drown,

VIII

So, to make all Rivals vain,
  Now I crown thee with my Love: **30**
Crown me with thy Love again,
  And we both shall Monarchs prove.

To his Coy Mistress

HAD we but World enough, and Time,
This coyness Lady were no crime.
We would sit down, and think which way
To walk, and pass our long Loves Day.
Thou by the *Indian Ganges* side   5
Should'st Rubies find: I by the Tide
Of *Humber* would complain. I would
Love you ten years before the Flood:
And you should if you please refuse
Till the Conversion of the *Jews*.   10
My vegetable Love should grow
Vaster then Empires, and more slow.
An hundred years should go to praise
Thine Eyes, and on thy Forehead Gaze.

Two hundred to adore each Breast: 15
But thirty thousand to the rest.
An Age at least to every part,
And the last Age should show your Heart.
For Lady you deserve this State;
Nor would I love at lower rate.   20
    But at my back I alwaies hear
Times winged Charriot hurrying near:
And yonder all before us lye
Desarts of vast Eternity.
Thy Beauty shall no more be found,   25
Nor, in thy marble Vault, shall sound
My ecchoing Song: then Worms shall try
That long preserv'd Virginity:
And your quaint Honour turn to dust;
And into ashes all my Lust.   30
The Grave's a fine and private place,
But none I think do there embrace.
    Now therefore, while the youthful hew
Sits on thy skin like morning dew,
And while thy willing Soul transpires   35
At every pore with instant Fires,
Now let us sport us while we may;
And now, like am'rous birds of prey,
Rather at once our Time devour,
Than languish in his slow-chapt pow'r.   40
Let us roll all our Strength, and all
Our sweetness, up into one Ball:
And tear our Pleasures with rough strife,
Thorough the Iron gates of Life.
Thus, though we cannot make our Sun   45
Stand still, yet we will make him run.

The Unfortunate Lover

I

ALAS, how pleasant are their dayes
With whom the Infant Love yet playes!
Sorted by pairs, they still are seen
By Fountains cool, and Shadows green.
But soon these Flames do lose their light,   **5**
Like Meteors of a Summers night:
Nor can they to that Region climb,
To make impression upon Time.

II

'Twas in a Shipwrack, when the Seas
Rul'd, and the Winds did what they please, **10**
That my poor Lover floting lay,
And, e're brought forth, was cast away:
Till at the last the master-Wave
Upon the Rock his Mother drave;
And there she split against the Stone,   **15**
In a *Cesarian Section*.

III

The Sea him lent these bitter Tears,
Which at his Eyes he alwaies bears.
And from the Winds the Sighs he bore,
Which through his surging Breast do roar. **20**
No Day he saw but that which breaks,
Through frighted Clouds in forked streaks.
While round the ratling Thunder hurl'd,
As at the Fun'ral of the World.

IV

While Nature to his Birth presents   **25**
This masque of quarrelling Elements;

A num'rous fleet of Corm'rants black,
That sail'd insulting o're the Wrack,
Receiv'd into their cruel Care,
Th' unfortunate and abject Heir: 30
Guardians most fit to entertain
The Orphan of the *Hurricane.*

V

They fed him up with Hopes and Air,
Which soon digested to Despair.
And as one Corm'rant fed him, still   35
Another on his Heart did bill.
Thus while they famish him, and feast,
He both consumed, and increast:
And languished with doubtful Breath,
Th' *Amphibium* of Life and Death.   40

VI

And now, when angry Heaven wou'd
Behold a spectacle of Blood,
Fortune and He are call'd to play
At sharp before it all the day:
And Tyrant Love his brest does ply   45
With all his wing'd Artillery.
Whilst he, betwixt the Flames and Waves,
Like *Ajax*, the mad Tempest braves.

VII

See how he nak'd and fierce does stand,
Cuffing the Thunder with one hand;   50
While with the other he does lock,
And grapple, with the stubborn Rock:
From which he with each Wave rebounds,
Torn into Flames, and ragg'd with Wounds.
And all he saies, a Lover drest   55
In his own Blood does relish best.

24

VIII

This is the only *Banneret*
That ever Love created yet:
Who though, by the Malignant Starrs,
Forced to live in Storms and Warrs;   60
Yet dying leaves a Perfume here,
And Musick within every Ear:
And he in Story only rules,
In a Field *Sable* a Lover *Gules*.

The Gallery

I

CLORA come view my Soul, and tell
Whether I have contriv'd it well.
Now all its several lodgings lye
Compos'd into one Gallery;
And the great *Arras*-hangings, made   5
Of various Faces, by are laid;
That, for all furniture, you'l find
Only your Picture in my Mind.

II

Here Thou art painted in the Dress
Of an Inhumane Murtheress;   10
Examining upon our Hearts
Thy fertile Shop of cruel Arts:
Engines more keen than ever yet
Adorned Tyrants Cabinet;
Of which the most tormenting are   15
Black Eyes, red Lips, and curled Hair.

III

But, on the other side, th' art drawn
Like to *Aurora* in the Dawn;
When in the East she slumb'ring lyes,
And stretches out her milky Thighs;   20
While all the morning Quire does sing,
And *Manna* falls, and Roses spring;
And, at thy Feet, the wooing Doves
Sit perfecting their harmless Loves.

IV

Like an Enchantress here thou show'st,   25
Vexing thy restless Lover's Ghost;
And, by a Light obscure, dost rave
Over his Entrails, in the Cave;
Divining thence, with horrid Care,
How long thou shalt continue fair;   30
And (when inform'd) them throw'st away,
To be the greedy Vultur's prey.

V

But, against that, thou sit'st a float
Like *Venus* in her pearly Boat.
The *Halcyons*, calming all that's nigh,   35
Betwixt the Air and Water fly.
Or, if some rowling Wave appears,
A Mass of Ambergris it bears.
Nor blows more Wind than what may well
Convoy the Perfume to the Smell.   40

VI

These Pictures and a thousand more,
Of Thee, my Gallery do store;
In all the Forms thou can'st invent
Either to please me, or torment:

For thou alone to people me,   45
Art grown a num'rous Colony;
And a Collection choicer far
Then or *White-hall's*, or *Mantua's* were.

VII

But, of these Pictures and the rest,
That at the Entrance likes me best: 50
Where the same Posture, and the Look
Remains, with which I first was took.
A tender Shepherdess, whose Hair
Hangs loosely playing in the Air,
Transplanting Flow'rs from the green Hill,   55
To crown her Head, and Bosome fill.

The Fair Singer

I

To make a final conquest of all me,
Love did compose so sweet an Enemy,
In whom both Beauties to my death agree,
Joyning themselves in fatal Harmony;   4
That while she with her Eyes my Heart does bind,
She with her Voice might captivate my Mind.

II

I could have fled from One but singly fair:
My dis-intangled Soul it self might save,
Breaking the curled trammels of her hair.
But how should I avoid to be her Slave,   10
Whose subtile Art invisibly can wreath
My Fetters of the very Air I breath?

III

It had been easy fighting in some plain,
Where Victory might hang in equal choice.
But all resistance against her is vain,   15
Who has th' advantage both of Eyes and Voice.
And all my Forces needs must be undone,
She having gained both the Wind and Sun.

Mourning

I

YOU, that decipher out the Fate
Of humane Off-springs from the Skies,
What mean these Infants which of late
Spring from the Starrs of *Chlora's* Eyes?

II

Her Eyes confus'd, and doubled ore,   5
With Tears suspended ere they flow;
Seem bending upwards, to restore
To Heaven, whence it came, their Woe.

III

When, molding of the watry Sphears,
Slow drops unty themselves away;   10
As if she, with those precious Tears,
Would strow the ground where *Strephon* lay.

IV

Yet some affirm, pretending Art,
Her Eyes have so her Bosome drown'd,
Only to soften near her Heart   15
A place to fix another Wound.

V

And, while vain Pomp does her restrain
Within her solitary Bowr,
She courts her self in am'rous Rain;
Her self both *Danae* and the Showr.　　　20

VI

Nay others, bolder, hence esteem
Joy now so much her Master grown,
That whatsoever does but seem
Like Grief, is from her Windows thrown.

VII

Nor that she payes, while she survives,　　　25
To her dead Love this Tribute due;
But casts abroad these Donatives,
At the installing of a new.

VIII

How wide they dream! The *Indian* Slaves
That sink for Pearl through Seas profound,　30
Would find her Tears yet deeper Waves
And not of one the bottom sound.

IX

I yet my silent Judgment keep,
Disputing not what they believe:
But sure as oft as Women weep,　　　35
It is to be suppos'd they grieve.

Daphnis and Chloe

I

DAPHNIS must from *Chloe* part:
Now is come the dismal Hour
That must all his Hopes devour,
All his Labour, all his Art.

II

Nature, her own Sexes foe,   5
Long had taught her to be coy:
But she neither knew t'enjoy,
Nor yet let her Lover go.

III

But, with this sad News surpriz'd,
Soon she let that Niceness fall;   10
And would gladly yield to all,
So it had his stay compriz'd.

IV

Nature so her self does use
To lay by her wonted State,
Lest the World should separate;   15
Sudden Parting closer glews.

V

He, well read in all the wayes
By which men their Siege maintain,
Knew not that the Fort to gain
Better 'twas the Siege to raise.   20

VI

But he came so full possest
With the Grief of Parting thence,
That he had not so much Sence
As to see he might be blest.

VII

Till Love in her Language breath'd   25
Words she never spake before;
But then Legacies no more
To a dying Man bequeath'd.

VIII

For, Alas, the time was spent,
Now the latest minut's run   30
When poor *Daphnis* is undone,
Between Joy and Sorrow rent.

IX

At that *Why*, that *Stay my Dear*,
His disorder'd Locks he tare;
And with rouling Eyes did glare,   35
And his cruel fate forswear.

X

As the Soul of one scarce dead,
With the shrieks of Friends aghast,
Looks distracted back in hast,
And then streight again is fled.   40

XI

So did wretched *Daphnis* look,
Frighting her he loved most.
At the last, this Lovers Ghost
Thus his Leave resolved took.

XII

Are my Hell and Heaven Joyn'd   **45**
More to torture him that dies?
Could departure not suffice,
But that you must then grow kind?

XIII

Ah my *Chloe* how have I
Such a wretched minute found,   **50**
When thy Favours should me wound
More than all thy Cruelty?

XIV

So to the condemned Wight
The delicious Cup we fill;
And allow him all he will,   **55**
For his last and short Delight.

XV

But I will not now begin
Such a Debt unto my Foe;
Nor to my Departure owe
What my Presence could not win.   **60**

XVI

Absence is too much alone:
Better 'tis to go in peace,
Than my Losses to increase
By a late Fruition.

XVII

Why should I enrich my Fate?   **65**
'Tis a Vanity to wear,
For my Executioner,
Jewels of so high a rate.

XVIII

Rather I away will pine
In a manly stubborness   **70**
Than be fatted up express
For the *Canibal* to dine.

XIX

Whilst this grief does thee disarm,
All th' Enjoyment of our Love
But the ravishment would prove   **75**
Of a Body dead while warm.

XX

And I parting should appear
Like the Gourmand *Hebrew* dead,
While with Quailes and *Manna* fed,
He does through the Desert err.   **80**

XXI

Or the Witch that midnight wakes
For the Fern, whose magick Weed
In one minute casts the Seed,
And invisible him makes.

XXII

Gentler times for Love are ment: **85**
Who for parting pleasure strain
Gather Roses in the rain,
Wet themselves and spoil their Scent.

XXIII

Farewel therefore all the fruit
Which I could from Love receive: **90**
Joy will not with Sorrow weave,
Nor will I this Grief pollute.

XXIV

Fate I come, as dark, as sad,
As thy Malice could desire;
Yet bring with me all the Fire 95
That Love in his Torches had.

XXV

At these words away he broke;
As who long has praying ly'n,
To his Heads-man makes the Sign,
And receives the parting stroke. 100

XXVI

But hence Virgins all beware.
Last night he with *Phlogis* slept;
This night for *Dorinda* kept;
And but rid to take the Air.

XXVII

Yet he does himself excuse; 105
Nor indeed without a Cause.
For, according to the Lawes,
Why did *Chloe* once refuse?

The Definition of Love

I

My Love is of a birth as rare
As 'tis for object strange and high:
It was begotten by despair
Upon Impossibility.

II

Magnanimous Despair alone   5
Could show me so divine a thing,
Where feeble Hope could ne'r have flown
But vainly flapt its Tinsel Wing.

III

And yet I quickly might arrive
Where my extended Soul is fixt,   10
But Fate does Iron wedges drive,
And alwaies crouds it self betwixt.

IV

For Fate with jealous Eye does see
Two perfect Loves; nor lets them close:
Their union would her ruine be,   15
And her Tyrannick pow'r depose.

V

And therefore her Decrees of Steel
Us as the distant Poles have plac'd,
(Though Loves whole World on us doth wheel)
Not by themselves to be embrac'd.   20

VI

Unless the giddy Heaven fall,
And Earth some new Convulsion tear;
And, us to joyn, the World should all
Be cramp'd into a *Planisphere*.

VII

As Lines so Loves *oblique* may well   25
Themselves in every Angle greet:
But ours so truly *Paralel*,
Though infinite can never meet.

VIII

Therefore the Love which us doth bind,
But Fate so enviously debarrs,   **30**
Is the Conjunction of the Mind,
And Opposition of the Stars.

The Picture of little T. C. in a
Prospect of Flowers

I

SEE with what simplicity
This Nimph begins her golden daies!
In the green Grass she loves to lie,
And there with her fair Aspect tames
The Wilder flow'rs, and gives them names: **5**
But only with the Roses playes;
             And them does tell
What Colour best becomes them, and what Smell.

II

Who can foretel for what high cause
This Darling of the Gods was born!   **10**
Yet this is She whose chaster Laws
The wanton Love shall one day fear,
And, under her command severe,
See his Bow broke and Ensigns torn.
           Happy, who can   **15**
Appease this virtuous Enemy of Man!

III

O then let me in time compound,
And parly with those conquering Eyes;
Ere they have try'd their force to wound,

36

Ere, with their glancing wheels, they drive   **20**
In Triumph over Hearts that strive,
And them that yield but more despise.
        Let me be laid,
Where I may see thy Glories from some Shade.

IV

Mean time, whilst every verdant thing   **25**
It self does at thy Beauty charm,
Reform the errours of the Spring;
Make that the Tulips may have share
Of sweetness, seeing they are fair;
And Roses of their thorns disarm;   **30**
        But most procure
That Violets may a longer Age endure.

V

But O young beauty of the Woods,
Whom Nature courts with fruits and flow'rs,
Gather the Flow'rs, but spare the Buds;   **35**
Lest *Flora* angry at thy crime,
To kill her Infants in their prime,
Do quickly make th' Example Yours;
        And, ere we see,
Nip in the blossome all our hopes and Thee.   **40**

Tom May's Death

As one put drunk into the Packet-boat,
Tom May was hurry'd hence and did not know't.
But was amaz'd on the Elysian side,
And with an Eye uncertain, gazing wide,
Could not determine in what place he was,   **5**
For whence in Stevens ally Trees or Grass?

Nor where the Popes head, nor the Mitre lay,
Signs by which still he found and lost his way.
At last while doubtfully he all compares,
He saw near hand, as he imagin'd *Ares*. 10
Such did he seem for corpulence and port,
But 'twas a man much of another sort;
'Twas *Ben* that in the dusky Laurel shade
Amongst the Chorus of old Poets laid,
Sounding of ancient Heroes, such as were 15
The Subjects Safety, and the Rebel's Fear.
But how a double headed Vulture Eats,
Brutus and *Cassius* the Peoples cheats.
But seeing *May* he varied streight his Song,
Gently to signifie that he was wrong. 20
Cups more then civil of *Emathian* wine,
I sing (said he) and the *Pharsalian* Sign,
Where the Historian of the Common-wealth
In his own Bowels sheath'd the conquering health.
By this *May* to himself and them was come, 25
He found he was translated, and by whom.
Yet then with foot as stumbling as his tongue
Prest for his place among the Learned throng.
But *Ben*, who knew not neither foe nor friend,
Sworn Enemy to all that do pretend, 30
Rose more than ever he was seen severe,
Shook his gray locks, and his own Bayes did tear
At this intrusion. Then with Laurel wand,
The awful Sign of his supream command.
At whose dread Whisk *Virgil* himself does quake,
And *Horace* patiently its stroke does take, 36
As he crowds in he whipt him ore the pate
Like *Pembroke* at the Masque, and then did rate.

Far from these blessed shades tread back agen
Most servil' wit, and Mercenary Pen. 40
Polydore, *Lucan*, *Allan*, *Vandale*, *Goth*,
Malignant Poet and Historian both.
Go seek the novice Statesmen, and obtrude

On them some Romane cast similitude,
Tell them of Liberty, the Stories fine,   45
Until you all grow Consuls in your wine.
Or thou *Dictator* of the glass bestow
On him the *Cato*, this the *Cicero*.
Transferring old *Rome* hither in your talk,
As *Bethlem's* House did to *Loretto* walk.   50
Foul Architect that hadst not Eye to see
How ill the measures of these States agree.
And who by *Romes* example *England* lay,
Those but to *Lucan* do continue *May*.
But the nor Ignorance nor seeming good   55
Misled, but malice fixt and understood.
Because some one than thee more worthy weares
The sacred Laurel, hence are all these teares?
Must therefore all the World be set on flame,
Because a Gazet writer mist his aim?   60
And for a Tankard-bearing Muse must we
As for the Basket *Guelphs* and *Gibellines* be?
When the Sword glitters ore the Judges head,
And fear has Coward Churchmen silenced,
Then is the Poets time, 'tis then he drawes,   65
And single fights forsaken Vertues cause.
He, when the wheel of Empire, whirleth back,
And though the World's disjointed Axel crack,
Sings still of ancient Rights and better Times,
Seeks wretched good, arraigns successful Crimes.
But thou base man first prostituted hast   71
Our spotless knowledge and the studies chast.
Apostatizing from our Arts and us,
To turn the Chronicler to *Spartacus*.
Yet wast thou taken hence with equal fate,   75
Before thou couldst great *Charles* his death relate.
But what will deeper wound thy little mind,
Hast left surviving *Davenant* still behind
Who laughs to see in this thy death renew'd,
Right Romane poverty and gratitude.   80

Poor Poet thou, and grateful Senate they,
Who thy last Reckoning did so largely pay.
And with the publick gravity would come,
When thou hadst drunk thy last to lead thee home.
If that can be thy home where *Spencer* lyes   85
And reverend *Chaucer*, but their dust does rise
Against thee, and expels thee from their side,
As th' Eagles Plumes from other birds divide.
Nor here thy shade must dwell, Return, Return,
Where Sulphrey *Phlegeton* does ever burn.   90
The *Cerberus* with all his Jawes shall gnash,
Megæra thee with all her Serpents lash.
Thou rivited unto *Ixion's* wheel
Shalt break, and the perpetual Vulture feel.
'Tis just what Torments Poets ere did feign,   95
Thou first Historically shouldst sustain.
 Thus by irrevocable Sentence cast,
 May only Master of these Revels past.
 And streight he vanisht in a Cloud of pitch,
 Such as unto the Sabboth bears the Witch.   100

The Match

I

NATURE had long a Treasure made
 Of all her choisest store;
Fearing, when She should be decay'd
 To beg in vain for more.

II

Her *Orientest* Colours there,   5
 And Essences most pure,
With sweetest Perfumes hoarded were,
 All as she thought secure.

III

She seldom them unlock'd, or us'd,
  But with the nicest care;   10
For, with one grain of them diffus'd,
  She could the World repair.

IV

But likeness soon together drew
  What she did separate lay;
Of which one perfect Beauty grew,   15
  And that was *Celia*.

V

Love wisely had of long fore-seen
  That he must once grow old;
And therefore stor'd a Magazine,
  To save him from the cold.   20

VI

He kept the several Cells repleat
  With Nitre thrice refin'd;
The Naphta's and the Sulphurs heat,
  And all that burns the Mind.

VII

He fortifi'd the double Gate,   25
  And rarely thither came;
For, with one Spark of these, he streight
  All Nature could inflame.

VIII

Till, by vicinity so long,
  A nearer Way they sought;   30
And, grown magnetically strong,
  Into each other wrought.

IX

Thus all his fewel did unite
　　To make one fire high:
None ever burn'd so hot, so bright:　　**35**
　　And *Celia* that am **I**.

X

So we alone the happy rest,
　　Whilst all the World is poor,
And have within our Selves possest
　　All Love's and Nature's store.　　**40**

The Mower against Gardens

Luxurious Man, to bring his Vice in use,
　　Did after him the World seduce:
And from the fields the Flow'rs and Plants allure,
　　Where Nature was most plain and pure.
He first enclos'd within the Gardens square　　5
　　A dead and standing pool of Air:
And a more luscious Earth for them did knead,
　　Which stupifi'd them while it fed.
The Pink grew then as double as his Mind;
　　The nutriment did change the kind.　　10
With strange perfumes he did the Roses taint.
　　And Flow'rs themselves were taught to paint.
The Tulip, white, did for complexion seek;
　　And learn'd to interline its cheek:
Its Onion root they then so high did hold,　　15
　　That one was for a Meadow sold.
Another World was search'd, through Oceans new,
　　To find the *Marvel of Peru*.
And yet these Rarities might be allow'd,
　　To Man, that sov'raign thing and proud;　　20

Had he not dealt between the Bark and Tree,
  Forbidden mixtures there to see.
No Plant now knew the Stock from which it came;
  He grafts upon the Wild the Tame:
That the uncertain and adult'rate fruit   25
  Might put the Palate in dispute.
His green *Seraglio* has its Eunuchs too;
  Lest any Tyrant him out-doe.
And in the Cherry he does Nature vex,
  To procreate without a Sex.   30
'Tis all enforc'd; the Fountain and the Grot;
  While the sweet Fields do lye forgot:
Where willing Nature does to all dispence
  A wild and fragrant Innocence:
And *Fauns* and *Faryes* do the Meadows till,   35
  More by their presence then their skill.
Their Statues polish'd by some ancient hand,
  May to adorn the Gardens stand:
But howso'ere the Figures do excel,
  The *Gods* themselves with us do dwell.   40

Damon the Mower

I

HEARK how the Mower *Damon* Sung,
With love of *Juliana* stung!
While ev'ry thing did seem to paint
The Scene more fit for his complaint.
Like her fair Eyes the day was fair;   5
But scorching like his am'rous Care.
Sharp like his Sythe his Sorrow was,
And wither'd like his Hopes the Grass.

II

Oh what unusual Heats are here,
Which thus our Sun-burn'd Meadows sear! 10
The Grass-hopper its pipe gives ore;
And hamstring'd Frogs can dance no more.
But in the brook the green Frog wades;
And Grass-hoppers seek out the shades.
Only the Snake, that kept within,   15
Now glitters in its second skin.

III

This heat the Sun could never raise,
Nor Dog-star so inflame's the dayes.
It from an higher Beauty grow'th,
Which burns the Fields and Mower both: 20
Which made the Dog, and makes the Sun
Hotter then his own *Phaeton*.
Not *July* causeth these Extremes,
But *Juliana's* scorching beams.

IV

Tell me where I may pass the Fires   25
Of the hot day, or hot desires.
To what cool Cave shall I descend,
Or to what gelid Fountain bend?
Alas! I look for Ease in vain,
When Remedies themselves complain.   30
No moisture but my Tears do rest,
Nor Cold but in her Icy Breast.

V

How long wilt Thou, fair Shepheardess,
Esteem me, and my Presents less?
To Thee the harmless Snake I bring,   35
Disarmed of its teeth and sting.

44

To Thee *Chameleons* changing-hue,
And Oak leaves tipt with hony due.
Yet Thou ungrateful hast not sought
Nor what they are, nor who them brought.   40

VI

I am the Mower *Damon*, known
Through all the Meadows I have mown.
On me the Morn her dew distills
Before her darling Daffadils.
And, if at Noon my toil me heat,   45
The Sun himself licks off my Sweat.
While, going home, the Ev'ning sweet
In cowslip-water bathes my feet.

VII

What, though the piping Shepherd stock
The plains with an unnum'red Flock,   50
This Sithe of mine discovers wide
More ground then all his Sheep do hide.
With this the golden fleece I shear
Of all these Closes ev'ry Year.
And though in Wooll more poor then they,   55
Yet am I richer far in Hay.

VIII

Nor am I so deform'd to sight,
If in my Sithe I looked right;
In which I see my Picture done,
As in a crescent Moon the Sun.   60
The deathless Fairyes take me oft
To lead them in their Danses soft:
And, when I tune my self to sing,
About me they contract their Ring.

IX

How happy might I still have mow'd,   65
Had not Love here his Thistles sow'd!
But now I all the day complain,
Joyning my Labour to my Pain;
And with my Sythe cut down the Grass,
Yet still my Grief is where it was: 70
But, when the Iron blunter grows,
Sighing I whet my Sythe and Woes.

X

While thus he threw his Elbow round,
Depopulating all the Ground,
And, with his whistling Sythe, does cut   75
Each stroke between the Earth and Root,
The edged Stele by careless chance
Did into his own Ankle glance;
And there among the Grass fell down,
By his own Sythe, the Mower mown.   80

XI

Alas! said He, these hurts are slight
To those that dye by Loves despight.
With Shepherds-purse, and Clowns-all-heal,
The Blood I stanch, and Wound I seal.
Only for him no Cure is found,   85
Whom *Julianas* Eyes do wound.
'Tis death alone that this must do:
For Death thou art a Mower too.

The Mower to the Glo-Worms

I

Ye living Lamps, by whose dear light
The Nightingale does sit so late,
And studying all the Summer-night,
Her matchless Songs does meditate;

II

Ye Country Comets, that portend   *5*
No War, nor Prince's funeral,
Shining unto no higher end
Then to presage the Grasses fall;

III

Ye Glo-worms, whose officious Flame
To wandring Mowers shows the way,   10
That in the Night have lost their aim,
And after foolish Fires do stray;

IV

Your courteous Lights in vain you wast,
Since *Juliana* here is come,
For She my Mind hath so displac'd   15
That I shall never find my home.

The Mower's Song

I

My Mind was once the true survey
Of all these Medows fresh and gay;
And in the greenness of the Grass
Did see its Hopes as in a Glass;

47

When *Juliana* came, and She   5
What I do to the Grass, does to my Thoughts and Me.

II

But these, while I with Sorrow pine,
Grew more luxuriant still and fine;
That not one Blade of Grass you spy'd,
But had a Flower on either side;   10
When *Juliana* came, and She
What I do to the Grass, does to my Thoughts and Me.

III

Unthankful Medows, could you so
A fellowship so true forego,
And in your gawdy May-games meet,   15
While I lay trodden under feet?
When *Juliana* came, and She
What I do to the Grass, does to my Thoughts and Me.

IV

But what you in Compassion ought,
Shall now by my Revenge be wrought: 20
And Flowr's, and Grass, and I and all,
Will in one common Ruine fall.
For *Juliana* comes, and She
What I do to the Grass, does to my Thoughts and Me.

V

And thus, ye Meadows, which have been   25
Companions of my thoughts more green,
Shall now the Heraldry become
With which I shall adorn my Tomb;
For *Juliana* comes, and She   29
What I do to the Grass, does to my Thoughts and Me.

Ametas and Thestylis making Hay-Ropes

I

Ametas

THINK'ST Thou that this Love can stand,
Whilst Thou still dost say me nay?
Love unpaid does soon disband:
Love binds Love as Hay binds Hay.

II

Thestylis

Think'st Thou that this Rope would twine   5
If we both should turn one way?
Where both parties so combine,
Neither Love will twist nor Hay.

III

Ametas

Thus you vain Excuses find,
Which your selve and us delay: 10
And Love tyes a Womans Mind
Looser then with Ropes of Hay.

IV

Thestylis

What you cannot constant hope
Must be taken as you may.

V

Ametas

Then let's both lay by our Rope,   15
And go kiss within the Hay.

Musicks Empire

I

FIRST was the World as one great Cymbal made,
Where Jarring Windes to infant Nature plaid.
All Musick was a solitary sound,
To hollow Rocks and murm'ring Fountains bound.

II

Jubal first made the wilder Notes agree;   5
And *Jubal* tuned Musicks *Jubilee*:
He call'd the *Ecchoes* from their sullen Cell,
And built the Organs City where they dwell.

III

Each sought a consort in that lovely place;
And Virgin Trebles wed the manly Base.   10
From whence the Progeny of numbers new
Into harmonious Colonies withdrew.

IV

Some to the Lute, some to the Viol went,
And others chose the Cornet eloquent.
These practising the Wind, and those the Wire,   15
To sing Mens Triumphs, or in Heavens quire.

V

Then Musick, the Mosaique of the Air,
Did of all these a solemn noise prepare:
With which She gain'd the Empire of the Ear,
Including all between the Earth and Sphear.   20

VI

Victorious sounds! yet here your Homage do
Unto a gentler Conqueror then you;
Who though He flies the Musick of his praise,
Would with you Heavens Hallelujahs raise

The Garden

I

How vainly men themselves amaze
To win the Palm, the Oke, or Bayes;
And their uncessant Labours see
Crown'd from some single Herb or Tree,
Whose short and narrow verged Shade   5
Does prudently their Toyles upbraid;
While all Flow'rs and all Trees do close
To weave the Garlands of repose.

II

Fair quiet, have I found thee here,
And Innocence thy Sister dear!   10
Mistaken long, I sought you then
In busie Companies of Men.
Your sacred Plants, if here below,
Only among the Plants will grow.
Society is all but rude,   15
To this delicious Solitude.

III

No white nor red was ever seen
So am'rous as this lovely green.
Fond Lovers, cruel as their Flame,
Cut in these Trees their Mistress name.   20

51

Little, Alas, they know, or heed,
How far these Beauties Hers exceed!
Fair Trees! where s'eer your barkes I wound,
No Name shall but your own be found.

IV

When we have run our Passions heat,   25
Love hither makes his best retreat.
The *Gods*, that mortal Beauty chase.
Still in a Tree did end their race.
Apollo hunted *Daphne* so,
Only that She might Laurel grow.   30
And *Pan* did after *Syrinx* speed,
Not as a Nymph, but for a Reed.

V

What wond'rous Life in this I lead!
Ripe Apples drop about my head;
The Luscious Clusters of the Vine   35
Upon my Mouth do crush their Wine;
The Nectaren, and curious Peach,
Into my hands themselves do reach;
Stumbling on Melons, as I pass,
Insnar'd with Flow'rs, I fall on Grass.   40

VI

Mean while the Mind, from pleasure less,
Withdraws into its happiness:
The Mind, that Ocean where each kind
Does streight its own resemblance find;
Yet it creates, transcending these,   45
Far other Worlds, and other Seas;
Annihilating all that's made
To a green Thought in a green Shade.

VII

Here at the Fountains sliding foot,
Or at some Fruit-trees mossy root,   50
Casting the Bodies Vest aside,
My Soul into the boughs does glide:
There like a Bird it sits, and sings,
Then whets, and combs its silver Wings;
And, till prepar'd for longer flight,   55
Waves in its Plumes the various Light.

VIII

Such was that happy Garden-state,
While Man there walk'd without a Mate:
After a Place so pure, and sweet,
What other Help could yet be meet!   60
But 'twas beyond a Mortal's share
To wander solitary there:
Two Paradises 'twere in one
To live in Paradise alone.

IX

How well the skilful Gardner drew   65
Of flow'rs and herbes this Dial new;
Where from above the milder Sun
Does through a fragrant Zodiack run;
And, as it works, th' industrious Bee
Computes its time as well as we.   70
How could such sweet and wholsome Hours
Be reckon'd but with herbs and flow'rs!

Hortus

QUISNAM adeo, mortale genus, præcordia versat?
Heu Palmæ, Laurique furor, vel simplicis Herbæ!
Arbor ut indomitos ornet vix una labores;
Tempora nec foliis præcingat tota malignis.
Dum simul implexi, tranquillæ ad serta Quiætis,   5
Omnigeni coeunt Flores, integraque Sylva.

   Alma Quies, teneo te! & te Germana Quietis
Simplicitas! Vos ergo diu per Templa, per urbes,
Quæsivi, Regum perque alta Palatia frustra.
Sed vos Hortorum per opaca silentia longe   10
Celarant Plantæ virides, & concolor Umbra.

   O! mihi si vestros liceat violasse recessus
Erranti, lasso, & vitæ melioris anhelo,
Municipem servate novum, votoque potitum,
Frondosæ Cives optate in florea Regna.   15

   Me quoque, vos *Musæ*, &, te conscie testor *Apollo*,
Non Armenta juvant hominum, *Circique* boatus,
Mugitusve Fori; sed me Penetralia veris,
Horroresque trahunt muti, & Consortia sola.

   Virgineæ quem non suspendit Gratia formæ?   20
Quam candore Nives vincentem, Ostrumque rubore,
Vestra tamen viridis superet (me judice) Virtus.
Nec foliis certare Comæ, nec Brachia ramis,
Nec possint tremulos voces æquare susurros.

   Ah quoties sævos vidi (quis credat?) Amantes   25
Sculpentes Dominæ potiori in cortice nomen?
Nec puduit truncis inscribere vulnera sacris,
Ast Ego, si vestras unquam temeravero stirpes,
Nulla *Neæra*, *Chloe*, *Faustina*, *Corynna*, legetur:
In proprio sed quæque libro signabitur Arbos.   30
O charæ *Platanus*, *Cyparissus*, *Populus*, *Ulmus*!

   Hic Amor, exutis crepidatus inambulat alis,
Enerves arcus & stridula tela reponens,
Invertitque faces, nec se cupit usque timeri;

Aut exporrectus jacet, indormitque pharetræ;   35
Non auditurus quanquam Cytherea vocarit;
Nequitias referunt nec somnia vana priores.
  Lætantur *Superi*, defervescente Tyranno,
Et licet experti toties *Nymphasque Deasque*,
Arbore nunc melius potiuntur quisque cupita.   40
Jupiter annosam, neglecta conjuge, *Quercum*
Deperit; haud alia doluit sic pellice *Juno*.
Lemniacum temerant vestigia nulla Cubile,
Nec *Veneris* Mavors meminit si *Fraxinus* adsit.
Formosæ pressit *Daphnes* vestigia *Phœbus*   45
Ut fieret *Laurus*; sed nil quæsiverat ultra.
Capripes & peteret quòd *Pan Syringa* fugacem,
Hoc erat ut *Calamum* posset reperire Sonorum.

Desunt multa

Nec tu, Opifex horti, grato sine carmine abibis:
Qui brevibus plantis, & læto flore, notasti   50
Crescentes horas, atque intervalla diei.
Sol ibi candidior fragrantia Signa pererrat;
Proque truci *Tauro*, stricto pro forcipe *Cancri*,
Securis violæque rosæque allabitur umbris.
Sedula quin & Apis, mellito intenta labori,   55
Horologo sua pensa thymo Signare videtur.
Temporis O suaves lapsus! O Otia sana!
  O Herbis dignæ numerari & Floribus Horæ!

To a Gentleman
that only upon the sight of
the Author's writing,
had given a Character of his
Person and Judgment of his Fortune

Illustrissimo Viro

Domino Lanceloto Josepho de Maniban

Grammatomanti

Quis posthac chartæ committat sensa loquaci,
    Si sua crediderit Fata subesse stylo?
Conscia si prodat Scribentis Litera sortem,
    Quicquid & in vita plus latuisse velit?
Flexibus in calami tamen omnia sponte leguntur   **5**
    Quod non significant Verba, Figura notat.
Bellerophonteas signat sibi quisque Tabellas;
    Ignaramque Manum Spiritus intus agit.
Nil præter solitum sapiebat Epistola nostra,
    Exemplumque meæ Simplicitatis erat.   **10**
Fabula jucundos qualis delectat Amicos;
    Urbe, lepore, novis, carmine tota scatens.
Hic tamen interpres quo non securior alter,
    (Non res, non voces, non ego notus ei)
Rimatur fibras notularum cautus Aruspex,   **15**
    Scripturæque inhians consulit exta meæ.
Inde statim vitæ casus, animique recessus
    Explicat; (haud *Genio* plura liquere putem.)
Distribuit totum nostris eventibus orbem,
    Et quo me rapiat cardine *Sphæra* docet.   **20**
Quæ *Sol* oppositus, quæ *Mars* adversa minetur,
    Jupiter aut ubi me, *Luna*, *Venusque* juvent.
Ut trucis intentet mihi vulnera *Cauda Draconis*;
    Vipereo levet ut vulnera more Caput.

Hinc mihi præteriti rationes atque futuri   25
    Elicit; *Astrologus* certior *Astronomo*.
Ut conjecturas nequeam discernere vero,
    Historiæ superet sed Genitura fidem.
Usque adeo cæli respondet pagina nostræ,
    Astrorum & nexus syllaba scripta refert.   30
Scilicet & toti subsunt Oracula mundo,
    Dummodo tot foliis una *Sibylla* foret.
Partum, Fortunæ mater Natura, propinquum
    Mille modis monstrat mille per indicia:
Ingentemque Uterum quâ mole Puerpera solvat; 35
    Vivit at in præsens maxima pars hominum.
Ast Tu sorte tuâ gaude Celeberrime Vatum;
    Scribe, sed haud superest qui tua fata legat.
Nostra tamen si fas præsagia jungere vestris,
    Quo magis inspexti sydera spernis humum.   40
Et, nisi stellarum fueris divina propago,
    Naupliada credam te *Palamede* satum.
Qui dedit ex avium scriptoria signa volatu,
    Sydereaque idem nobilis arte fuit.
Hinc utriusque tibi cognata scientia crevit,   45
    Nec minus augurium Litera quam dat Avis.

Fleckno, an English Priest at Rome

OBLIG'D by frequent visits of this man,
Whom as Priest, Poet, and Musician,
I for some branch of *Melchizedeck* took,
(Though he derives himself from *my Lord Brooke*)
I sought his Lodging; which is at the Sign   5
Of the sad *Pelican*; Subject divine
For Poetry: There three Stair-Cases high,
Which signifies his triple property,
I found at last a Chamber, as 'twas said,
But seem'd a Coffin set on the Stairs head.   10

Not higher than Seav'n, nor larger then three feet;
Only there was nor Seeling, nor a Sheet,
Save that th' ingenious Door did as you come
Turn in, and shew to Wainscot half the Room.
Yet of his State no man could have complain'd;   15
There being no Bed where he entertain'd:
And though within one Cell so narrow pent,
He'd *Stanza's* for a whole Appartement.
    Straight without further information,
In hideous verse, he, and a dismal tone,   20
Begins to exorcise; as if I were
Possest; and sure the *Devil* brought me there.
But I, who now imagin'd my self brought
To my last Tryal, in a serious thought
Calm'd the disorders of my youthful Breast,   25
And to my Martyrdom prepared Rest.
Only this frail Ambition did remain,
The last distemper of the sober Brain,
That there had been some present to assure
The future Ages how I did indure: 30
And how I, silent, turn'd my burning Ear
Towards the Verse; and when that could not hear,
Held him the other; and unchanged yet,
Ask'd still for more, and pray'd him to repeat:
Till the Tyrant, weary to persecute,   35
Left off, and try'd t' allure me with his Lute.
    Now as two Instruments, to the same key
Being tun'd by Art, if the one touched be
The other opposite as soon replies,
Mov'd by the Air and hidden Sympathies;   40
So while he with his gouty Fingers craules
Over the Lute, his murmuring Belly calls,
Whose hungry Guts to the same streightness twin'd
In Echo to the trembling Strings repin'd.
    I, that perceiv'd now what his Musick ment,   45
Ask'd civilly if he had eat this Lent.

He answered yes; with such, and such an one.
For he has this of gen'rous, that alone
He never feeds; save only when he tryes
With gristly Tongue to dart the passing Flyes.   50
I ask'd if he eat flesh. And he, that was
So hungry that though ready to say *Mass*
Would break his fast before, said he was Sick,
And th' *Ordinance* was only Politick.
Nor was I longer to invite him: Scant   55
Happy at once to make him Protestant,
And Silent. Nothing now the Dinner stay'd
But till he had himself a Body made.
I mean till he were drest: for else so thin
He stands, as if he only fed had been   60
With consecrated Wafers: and the *Host*
Hath sure more flesh and blood then he can boast.
This *Basso Relievo* of a Man,
Who as a Camel tall, yet easly can
The Needles Eye thread without any stich,   65
(His only impossible is to be rich)
Lest his too suttle Body, growing rare,
Should leave his Soul to wander in the Air,
He therefore circumscribes himself in rimes;
And swaddled in's own papers seaven times,   70
Wears a close Jacket of poetick Buff,
With which he doth his third Dimension Stuff.
Thus armed underneath, he over all
Does make a primitive *Sotana* fall;
And above that yet casts an antick Cloak,   75
Worn at the first Counsel of *Antioch*;
Which by the *Jews* long hid, and Disesteem'd,
He heard of by Tradition, and redeem'd.
But were he not in this black habit deck't,
This half transparent Man would soon reflect   80
Each colour that he past by; and be seen.
As the *Chamelion*, yellow, blew, or green.

He drest, and ready to disfurnish now
His Chamber, whose compactness did allow
No empty place for complementing doubt,   85
But who came last is forc'd first to go out;
I meet one on the Stairs who made me stand,
Stopping the passage, and did him demand:
I answer'd he is here *Sir*; but you see
You cannot pass to him but thorow me.   90
He thought himself affronted; and reply'd,
I whom the Pallace never has deny'd
Will make the way here; I said *Sir* you'l do
Me a great favour, for I seek to go.
He gathring fury still made sign to draw;   95
But himself there clos'd in a Scabbard saw
As narrow as his Sword's; and I, that was
Delightful, said there can no Body pass
Except by penetration hither, where
Two make a crowd, nor can three Persons here 100
Consist but in one substance. Then, to fit
Our peace, the Priest said I too had some wit:
To prov't, I said, the place doth us invite
By its own narrowness, Sir, to unite.
He ask'd me pardon; and to make me way   105
Went down, as I him follow'd to obey.
But the propitiatory Priest had straight
Oblig'd us, when below, to celebrate
Together our attonement: so increas'd
Betwixt us two the Dinner to a Feast.   110
Let it suffice that we could eat in peace;
And that both Poems did and Quarrels cease
During the Table; though my new made Friend
Did, as he threatened, ere 'twere long intend
To be both witty and valiant: I loth,   115
Said 'twas too late, he was already both.

But now, Alas, my first Tormentor came,
Who satisfy'd with eating, but not tame

Turns to recite; though Judges most severe
After th' Assizes dinner mild appear,   120
And on full stomach do condemn but few:
Yet he more strict my sentence doth renew;
And draws out of the black box of his Breast
Ten quire of paper in which he was drest.
Yet that which was a greater cruelty   125
Then *Nero's* Poem he calls charity:
And so the *Pelican* at his door hung
Picks out the tender bosome to its young.
    Of all his Poems there he stands ungirt
Save only two foul copies for his shirt: 130
Yet these he promises as soon as clean.
But how I loath'd to see my Neighbour glean
Those papers, which he pilled from within
Like white fleaks rising from a Leaper's skin!
More odious then those raggs which the *French*
    youth   135
At ordinaries after dinner show'th,
When they compare their *Chancres* and *Poulains.*
Yet he first kist them, and after takes pains
To read; and then, because he understood
Not one Word, thought and swore that they were
    good.   140
But all his praises could not now appease
The provok't Author, whom it did displease
To hear his Verses, by so just a curse,
That were ill made condemn'd to be read worse:
And how (impossible) he made yet more   145
Absurdityes in them then were before.
For he his untun'd voice did fall or raise
As a deaf Man upon a Viol playes,
Making the half points and the periods run
Confus'der then the atomes in the Sun.   150
Thereat the Poet swell'd, with anger full,
And roar'd out, like *Perillus* in's own *Bull*;

61

Sir you read false. That any one but you
Should know the contrary. Whereat, I, now
Made Mediator, in my room, said, Why?   155
To say that you read false *Sir* is no Lye.
Thereat the waxen Youth relented straight;
But saw with sad dispair that 'twas too late.
For the disdainful Poet was retir'd
Home, his most furious Satyr to have fir'd   160
Against the Rebel; who, at this struck dead,
Wept bitterly as disinherited.
Who should commend his Mistress now? Or who
Praise him? both difficult indeed to do
With truth. I counsell'd him to go in time,   165
Ere the fierce Poets anger turn'd to rime.
    He hasted; and I, finding my self free,
As one scap't strangely from Captivity,
Have made the Chance be painted; and go now
To hang it in *Saint Peter's* for a Vow.   170

Dignissimo suo Amico Doctori Wittie

De Translatione Vulgi Errorum
D. Primrosii

NEMPE sic innumero succrescunt agmine libri,
    Sæpia vix toto ut jam natet una mari.
Fortius assidui surgunt a vulnere præli:
    Quoque magis pressa est, auctior Hydra redit.
Heu quibus Anticyris, quibus est sanabilis herbis 5
    Improba scribendi pestis, avarus amor!
India sola tenet tanti medicamina morbi,
    Dicitur & nostris ingemuisse malis.
Utile Tabacci dedit illa miserta venenum,
    Acri veratro quod meliora potest.   10
Jamque vides olidas libris fumare popinas:

Naribus O doctis quam pretiosus odor!
Hâc ego præcipua credo herbam dote placere,
    Hinc tuus has nebulas Doctor in astra vehit.
Ah mea quid tandem facies timidissima charta?   15
    Exequias Siticen jam parat usque tuas.
Hunc subeas librum Sancti ceu limen asyli,
    Quem neque delebit flamma, nec ira Jovis.

To his worthy Friend Doctor Witty upon his Translation of the Popular Errors

SIT further, and make room for thine own fame,
Where just desert enrolles thy honour'd Name
The good Interpreter. Some in this task
Take of the Cypress vail, but leave a mask,
Changing the Latine, but do more obscure   5
That sence in *English* which was bright and pure.
So of Translators they are Authors grown,
For ill Translators make the Book their own.
Others do strive with words and forced phrase
To add such lustre, and so many rayes,   10
That but to make the Vessel shining, they
Much of the precious Metal rub away.
He is Translations thief that addeth more,
As much as he that taketh from the Store
Of the first Author. Here he maketh blots   15
That mends; and added beauties are but spots.
    Cælia whose English doth more richly flow
Then *Tagus*, purer then dissolved snow,
And sweet as are her lips that speak it, she
Now learns the tongues of *France* and *Italy*;   20
But she is *Cælia* still: no other grace
But her own smiles commend that lovely face;

Her native beauty's not Italianated,
Nor her chast mind into the *French* translated:
Her thoughts are *English*, though her sparkling wit
With other Language doth them fitly fit.   26
    Translators learn of her: but stay I slide
Down into Error with the Vulgar tide;
Women must not teach here: the Doctor doth
Stint them to Cawdles, Almond-milk, and Broth.
Now I reform, and surely so will all   31
Whose happy Eyes on thy Translation fall,
I see the people hastning to thy Book,
Liking themselves the worse the more they look,
And so disliking, that they nothing see   35
Now worth the liking, but thy Book and thee.
And (if I Judgment have) I censure right;
For something guides my hand that I must write.
You have Translations statutes best fulfil'd.
That handling neither sully nor would guild.   40

On Mr. *Milton's* Paradise Lost

WHEN I beheld the Poet blind, yet bold,
In slender Book his vast Design unfold,
Messiah Crown'd, *Gods* Reconcil'd Decree,
Rebelling *Angels*, the Forbidden Tree,
Heav'n, Hell, Earth, Chaos, All; the Argument   5
Held me a while misdoubting his Intent,
That he would ruine (for I saw him strong)
The sacred Truths to Fable and old Song,
(So *Sampson* groap'd the Temples Posts in spight)
The World o'rewhelming to revenge his Sight.   10
    Yet as I read, soon growing less severe,
I lik'd his Project, the success did fear;
Through that wide Field how he his way should find
O're which lame Faith leads Understanding blind;

Lest he perplext the things he would explain,　　15
And what was easie he should render vain.
　Or if a Work so infinite he spann'd,
Jealous I was that some less skilful hand
(Such as disquiet alwayes what is well,
And by ill imitating would excell)　　20
Might hence presume the whole Creations day
To change in Scenes, and show it in a Play.
　Pardon me, *mighty Poet*, nor despise
My causeless, yet not impious, surmise.
But I am now convinc'd, and none will dare　　25
Within thy Labours to pretend a Share.
Thou hast not miss'd one thought that could be fit,
And all that was improper dost omit:
So that no room is here for Writers left,
But to detect their Ignorance or Theft.　　30
　That Majesty which through thy Work doth Reign
Draws the Devout, deterring the Profane.
And things divine thou treatst of in such state
As them preserves, and Thee inviolate.
At once delight and horrour on us seize,　　35
Thou singst with so much gravity and ease;
And above humane flight dost soar aloft,
With Plume so strong, so equal, and so soft.
The *Bird* nam'd from that *Paradise* you sing
So never Flags, but alwaies keeps on Wing.　　40
　Where couldst thou Words of such a compass find?
Whence furnish such a vast expense of Mind?
Just Heav'n Thee, like *Tiresias*, to requite,
Rewards with *Prophesie* thy loss of Sight.
　Well mightst thou scorn thy Readers to allure　　45
With tinkling Rhime, of thy own Sense secure;
While the *Town-Bays* writes all the while and spells,
And like a Pack-Horse tires without his Bells.
Their Fancies like our bushy Points appear,
The Poets tag them; we for fashion wear.　　50

I too transported by the *Mode* offend,
And while I meant to *Praise* thee, must Commend.
Thy verse created like thy *Theme* sublime,
In Number, Weight, and Measure, needs not *Rhime*.

Inscribenda Luparæ

CONSURGIT *Luparæ* Dum non imitabile culmen,
  Escuriale ingens uriter invidia.

Aliter

Regibus hæc posuit *Ludovicus* Templa futuris;
  Gratior ast ipsi *Castra* fuere Domus.

Aliter

Hanc sibi Sydeream *Ludovicus* condidit Aulam; 5
  Nec se propterea credidit esse *Deum*.

Aliter

Atria miraris, summotumque Æthera tecto;
  Nec tamen in toto est arctior Orbe Casa.

Aliter

Instituente domum *Ludovico*, prodiit Orbis;
  Sic tamen angustos incolit ille Lares.   10

Aliter

Sunt geminæ *Jani* Portæ, sunt Tecta *Tonantis*;
  Nec deerit *Numen* dum *Ludovicus* adest.

Upon an Eunuch; a Poet

Fragment

NEC sterilem te crede; licet, mulieribus exul,
Falcem virginiæ nequeas immitere messi,
Et nostro peccare modo. Tibi Fama perennè
Prægnabit; rapiesque novem de monte Sorores;
Et pariet modulos *Echo* repitita Nepotes.

In the French translation of Lucan, by Monsieur De Brebeuf are these Verses

C'EST de luy que nous vient cet Art ingenieux
De peindre la Parole, et de parler aux Yeux;
Et, par les traits divers de figures tracées,
Donner de la couleur et du corps aux pensées.

Translated

Facundis dedit ille notis, interprete pluma
Insinuare sonos oculis, & pingere voces,
Et mentem chartis, oculis impertiit aurem.

Senec. Traged. ex Thyeste Chor. 2

Stet quicunque volet potens
Aulæ culmine lubrico &c.

Translated

CLIMB at *Court* for me that will
Tottering favors Pinacle;

67

All I seek is to lye still.
Settled in some secret Nest
In calm Leisure let me rest;   5
And far off the publick Stage
Pass away my silent Age.
Thus when without noise, unknown,
I have liv'd out all my span,
I shall dye, without a groan,   10
An old honest Country man.
Who expos'd to others Ey's,
Into his own Heart ne'r pry's,
Death to him's a Strange surprise.

Janæ Oxenbrigiæ Epitaphium

JUXTA hoc Marmor, breve Mortalitatis speculum,
Exuviæ jacent Janæ Oxenbrigiæ. Quæ nobili, si id
dixisse attinet, paterno *Butleriorum,* materno
Claveringiorum genere orta, *Johanni Oxenbrigio*
Collegii hujus socio nupsit. Prosperorum deinceps   5
et adversorum ei Consors fidelissima. Quem, Reli-
gionis causa oberrantem, Usque ad incertam *Ber-
mudæ Insulam* secuta: Nec Mare vastum, nec
tempestates horridas exhorruit: sed, delicato Cor-
pore, quos non Labores exantlavit? quæ non, obivit 10
Itinera? Tantum *Mariti* potuit Amor, sed magis *Dei.*
Tandem cum, (redeunte conscientiarum libertate)
in patriam redux, magnam partem *Angliæ* cum
Marito pervagata; qui lætus undequaque de novo
disseminabat *Evangelium.* Ipsa maximum ministerii 15
sui decus, & antiqua modestia eandem animarum
capturam domi, quam ille foris exercens, hic tandem divino nutu cum illo consedit: Ubi pietatis
erga *Deum,* conjugalis & materni affectus, erga
proximos charitatis, omnium denique Virtutum 20

68

Christianarum Exemplum degebat inimitabile. Donec quinque annorum hydrope laborans, per lenta
incrementa ultra humani corporis modum intumuit.
Anima interim spei plena, fidei ingens, Stagnanti
humorum diluvio tranquillè vehebatur. Et tandem, 25
post 37. peregrinationis annos, 23 Apr. Anno 1658.
Evolavit ad Cœlos, tanquam Columba ex Arca
Corporis: Cujus semper dulci, semper amaræ
memoriæ, Mœrens Maritus posuit. Flentibus juxta
quatuor liberis, *Daniele, Bathshua, Elizabetha,* 30
Maria.

Johannis Trottii Epitaphium

CHARISSIMO Filio Iohanni Trottio
    Iohannes Trottius
(E Laverstoke In Agro Hantoniensi Baronettus)
Pater Et Elizabetha Mater
Funebrem tabulam curavimus.   5
  Age Marmor, & pro solita tua humanitate,
(Ne inter Parentum Dolorem & Modestiam
Supprimantur præclari Juvenis meritæ laudes)
    Effare *Johannis Trotii* breve Elogium.
    Erat ille totus Candidus, Politus, Solidus,   10
    Ultra vel Parii Marmoris metaphoram,
    Et Gemmâ Scalpi dignus, non Lapide:
E Schola *Wintoniensi* ad *Academiam Oxonii,*
Inde ad *Interioris Templi* Hospitium gradum fecerat:
Summæ Spei, Summæ Indolis, ubique vestigia reliquit;
    Supra Sexum Venustus,   16
    Supra Ætatem Doctus,
    Ingeniosus supra Fidem.
  Et jam vicesimum tertium annum inierat,
  Pulcherrimo undequaque vitæ prospectu,   20
    Quem Mors immatura obstruxit

Ferales Pustulæ Corpus tam affabre factum
Ludibrio habuere, & vivo incrustarunt sepulchro.
   Anima evasit Libera, Æterna, Fælix,
     Et morti insultans   25
   Mortalem Sortem cum Fænore accipiet.
   Nos interim, meri vespillones,
Parentes Filio extra ordinem Parentantes,
Subtus in gentilitia crypta reliquias composuimus,
   Ipsi eandem ad *Dei* nutum subituri.   30
   Natus est xxvii° Sept/^{is} An° MDCCXLII obiit
     xxviii° Junii MDCLXIIII
     Reviviscet Primo Resurrectionis.

To Sir John Trott

Honoured Sir,

I HAVE not that vanity to believe, if you weigh
your late Loss by the common ballance, that any
thing I can write to you should lighten your re-
sentments: nor if you measure things by the rule of
Christianity, do I think it needful to comfort you in 5
your own duty and your Sons happiness. Only having a great esteem and affection for you, and the
grateful memory of him that is departed being still
green and fresh upon my Spirit, I cannot forbear to
inquire how you have stood the second shock at 10
your sad meeting of Friends in the Country. I know
that the very sight of those who have been wit-
nesses of our better Fortune, doth but serve to re-
inforce a Calamity. I know the contagion of grief,
and infection of Tears, and especially when it runs 15
in a blood. And I my self could sooner imitate then
blame those innocent relentings of Nature, so that
they spring from tenderness only and humanity,
not from an implacable sorrow. The Tears of a

family may flow together like those little drops that 20
compact the Rainbow, and if they be plac'd with the
same advantage towards Heaven as those are to the
Sun, they too have their splendor: and like that bow
while they unbend into seasonable showers, yet they
promise that there shall not be a second flood. But 25
the dissoluteness of grief, the prodigality of sorrow
is neither to be indulg'd in a mans self, nor com-
ply'd within others. If that were allowable in these
cases, *Eli's* was the readiest way and highest com-
plement of mourning, who fell back from his seat 30
and broke his neck. But neither does that precedent
hold. For though he had been Chancellor, and in
effect King of *Israel*, for so many years; and such
men value as themselves so their losses at an higher
rate then others; yet when he heard that *Israel* was 35
overcome, that his two Sons *Hophni* and *Phineas*
were slain in one day, and saw himself so without
hope of Issue, and which imbittered it further without succession to the Government, yet he fell not
till the News that the Ark of God was taken. I pray 40
God that we may never have the same paralel per-
fected in our publick concernments. Then we shall
need all the strength of Grace and Nature to support us. But upon a private loss, and sweetned with
so many circumstances as yours, to be impatient, 45
to be uncomfortable, would be to dispute with God
and beg the question. Though in respect of an only
gourd an only Son be inestimable, yet in compari-
son to God man bears a thousand times less proportion: so that it is like *Jonah's* sin to be angry at 50
God for the withering of his Shadow. *Zipporah*,
though the delay had almost cost her husband his
life, yet when he did but circumcise her Son, in a
womanish pevishness reproacht *Moses* as a bloody
husband. But if God take the Son himself, but spare 55
the Father, shall we say that he is a bloody God.

He that gave his own Son, may he not take ours?"
'Tis pride that makes a Rebel. And nothing but the
over-weening of our selves and our own things that
raises us against divine Providence. Whereas *Abra-* 60
ham's obedience was better then Sacrifice. And if
God please to accept both, it is indeed a farther
Tryal, but a greater honour. I could say over upon
this beaten occasion most of those lessons of moral-
ity and religion that have been so often repeated and 65
are as soon forgotten. We abound with precept, but
we want examples. You, Sir, that have all these
things in your memory, and the clearness of whose
Judgment is not to be obscured by any greater inter-
position, it remains that you be exemplary to others 70
in your own practice. 'Tis true, it is an hard task to
learn and teach at the same time. And, where your
self are the experiment, it is as if a man should dis-
sect his own body and read the Anatomy Lecture.
But I will not heighten the difficulty while I advise 75
the attempt. Only, as in difficult things, you will do
well to make use of all that may strengthen and
assist you. The word of God: The society of good
men: and the books of the Ancients. There is one
way more, which is by diversion, business, and 80
activity; which are also necessary to be used in their
season. But I my self, who live to so little purpose,
can have little authority or ability to advise you in
it, who are a Person that are and may be much more
so generally useful. All that I have been able to do 85
since, hath been to write this sorry Elogie of your
Son, which if it be as good as I could wish, it is as
yet no undecent imployment. However, I know you
will take any thing kindly from your very affection-
ate friend and most humble Servant. 90

Edmundi Trotii Epitaphium

DILECTISSIMO Filio *Edmundo Trottio*
Posuimus Iidem Iohannes Pater Et Elizabetha Mater
      Frustra superstites.
Legite Parentes, vanissimus hominum ordo,
      Figuli Filiorum, Substructores Nominum, 5
      Fartores Opum, Longi Speratores,
Et nostro, si fas, sapite infortunio.
          Fuit *Edmundus Trottius.*
E quatuor masculæ stirpis residuus,
Statura justa, Forma virili, specie eximia, 10
Medio juventutis Robore simul & Flore,
Aspectu, Incessu, sermone juxta amabilis,
Et siquid ultra Cineri pretium addit.
      Honesta Disciplina domi imbutus,
          Peregre profectus 15
        Generosis Artibus Animum
        Et exercitiis Corpus firmaverat.
      Circæam Insulam, Scopulos *Sirenum*
          Præternavigavit,
      Et in hoc naufragio morum & sæculi 20
Solus perdiderat nihil, auxit plurimum.
          Hinc erga *Deum* pietate,
      Erga nos Amore & Obsequio,
Comitate erga Omnes, & intra se Modestia
      Insignis, & quantævis fortunæ capax: 25
      Delitiæ Æqualium, Senum Plausus,
      Oculi Parentum, (nunc, ah, Lachrymæ)
In eo tandem peccavit quòd mortalis.
      Et fatali Pustularum morbo aspersus,
          Factus est 30
(Ut veræ Laudis Invidiam ficto Convitio levemus)
      Proditor Amicorum, Parricida Parentum,
          Familiæ Spongia:

Et Naturæ invertens ordinem
             Nostri suique Contemptor,   35
            Mundi Desertor, deficit ad *Deum.*
Undecimo Augusti Æræ Christianæ 1667 suæ XXIIII
Talis quum fuerit Coelo non invidemus.

An Epitaph upon ——

HERE under rests the body of   , who in
his life-time reflected all the lustre he derived from
his Family, and recompens'd the Honour of his Des-
cent by his Virtue. For being of an excellent Nature,
he cultivated it nevertheless by all the best means 5
of improvement: nor left any spot empty for the
growth of Pride, or Vanity. So that, although he was
polished to the utmost perfection, he appeared only
as a Mirrour for others, not himself to look in.
Chearful without Gall, Sober without Formality, **10**
Prudent without Stratagem; and Religious without
Affectation. He neither neglected, nor yet pretended
to Business: but as he loved not to make work, so
not to leave it imperfect. He understood, but was
not enamour'd of Pleasure. He never came before **15**
in Injury, nor behind in Courtesie: nor found
sweetness in any Revenge but that of Gratitude.
He so studiously discharged the obligations of a
Subject, a Son, a Friend, and an Husband, as if
those relations could have consisted only on his **20**
part. Having thus walked upright, and easily
through this World, nor contributed by any excess
to his Mortality; yet Death took him: wherein
therefore, as his last Duty, he signaliz'd the more
his former Life with all the Decency and Recum- **25**
bence of a departing Christian.

An Epitaph upon ——

ENOUGH: and leave the rest to Fame.
'Tis to commend her but to name.
Courtship, which living she declin'd,
When dead to offer were unkind.
Where never any could speak ill,   5
Who would officious Praises spill?
Nor can the truest Wit or Friend,
Without Detracting, her commend.
To say she liv'd a *Virgin* chast,
In this Age loose and all unlac't;   10
Nor was, when Vice is so allow'd,
Of *Virtue* or asham'd, or proud;
That her Soul was on *Heaven* so bent
No Minute but it came and went;
That ready her last Debt to pay   15
She summ'd her Life up ev'ry day;
Modest as Morn; as Mid-day bright;
Gentle as Ev'ning; cool as Night;
'Tis true: but all so weakly said;
'Twere more Significant, *She's Dead.*   20

Epigramma in Duos montes Amosclivum Et Bilboreum. Farfacio

CERNIS ut ingenti distinguant limite campum
    Montis Amos clivi Bilboreique juga!
Ille stat indomitus turritis undique saxis:
    Cingit huic lætum Fraxinus alta Caput.
Illi petra minax rigidis cervicibus horret: 5
    Huic quatiunt virides lenia colla jubas.
Fulcit *Atlanteo* Rupes ea vertice cœlos:
    Collis at hic humeros subjicit *Herculeos.*

Hic ceu carceribus visum sylvaque coercet:
    Ille Oculos alter dum quasi meta trahit.   10
Ille Giganteum surgit ceu *Pelion Ossa*:
    Hic agit ut *Pindi* culmine *Nympha* choros.
Erectus, præceps, salebrosus, & arduus ille:
    Acclivis, placidus, mollis, amænus hic est.
Dissimilis Domino coiit Natura sub uno;   15
    Farfaciaque tremunt sub ditione pares.
Dumque triumphanti terras perlabitur Axe,
    Præteriens æqua stringit utrumque Rota.
Asper in adversos, facilis cedentibus idem;
    Ut credas Montes extimulasse suos.   20
Hi sunt *Alcidæ Borealis* nempe Columnæ,
    Quos medio scindit vallis opaca freto.
An potius, longe sic prona cacumina nutant,
    Parnassus cupiant esse *Maria* tuus.

Upon the Hill and Grove at Bill-borow

To the Lord Fairfax

I

SEE how the arched Earth does here
Rise in a perfect Hemisphere!
The stiffest Compass could not strike
A Line more circular and like;
Nor softest Pensel draw a Brow   5
So equal as this Hill does bow.
It seems as for a Model laid,
And that the World by it was made.

II

Here learn ye Mountains more unjust,
Which to abrupter greatness thrust,   10

That do with your hook-shoulder'd height
The Earth deform and Heaven fright.
For whose excrescence ill design'd,
Nature must a new Center find,
Learn here those humble steps to tread,   **15**
Which to securer Glory lead.

III

See what a soft access and wide
Lyes open to its grassy side;
Nor with the rugged path deterrs
The feet of breathless Travellers.   **20**
See then how courteous it ascends,
And all the way it rises bends;
Nor for it self the height does gain,
But only strives to raise the Plain.

IV

Yet thus it all the field commands,   **25**
And in unenvy'd Greatness stands,
Discerning further then the Cliff
Of Heaven-daring *Teneriff*.
How glad the weary Seamen hast
When they salute it from the Mast!   **30**
By Night the Northern Star their way
Directs, and this no less by Day.

V

Upon its crest this Mountain grave
A Plump of aged Trees does wave.
No hostile hand durst ere invade   **35**
With impious Steel the sacred Shade.
For something alwaies did appear
Of the *great Masters* terrour there:
And Men could hear his Armour still
Ratling through all the Grove and Hill.   **40**

VI

Fear of the *Master*, and respect
Of the great *Nymph* did it protect;
Vera the *Nymph* that him inspir'd,
To whom he often here retir'd,
And on these Okes ingrav'd her Name;   45
Such Wounds alone these Woods became:
But ere he well the Barks could part
'Twas writ already in their Heart.

VII

For they ('tis credible) have sense,
As Wc, of Love and Reverence,   50
And underneath the Courser Rind
The *Genius* of the house do bind.
Hence they successes seem to know,
And in their *Lord's* advancement grow;
But in no Memory were seen   55
As under this so streight and green.

VIII

Yet now no further strive to shoot,
Contented if they fix their Root.
Nor to the winds uncertain gust,
Their prudent Heads too far intrust.   60
Onely sometimes a flutt'ring Breez
Discourses with the breathing Trees;
Which in their modest Whispers name
Those Acts that swell'd the Cheek of Fame.

IX

Much other Groves, say they, then these   65
And other Hills him once did please.
Through Groves of Pikes he thunder'd then,
And Mountains rais'd of dying Men.

For all the *Civick Garlands* due
To him our Branches are but few.   70
Nor are our Trunks enow to bear
The *Trophees* of one fertile Year.

X

'Tis true, ye Trees nor ever spoke
More certain *Oracles* in Oak.
But Peace (if you his favour prize)   75
That Courage its own Praises flies.
Therefore to your obscurer Seats
From his own Brightness he retreats:
Nor he the Hills without the Groves,
Nor Height but with Retirement loves.   80

Upon Appleton House, to my Lord Fairfax

I

WITHIN this sober Frame expect
Work of no Forrain *Architect*;
That unto Caves the Quarries drew,
And Forrests did to Pastures hew;
Who of his great Design in pain   5
Did for a Model vault his Brain,
Whose Columnes should so high be rais'd
To arch the Brows that on them gaz'd.

II

Why should of all things Man unrul'd
Such unproportion'd dwellings build?   10
The Beasts are by their Denns exprest:
And Birds contrive an equal Nest;

The low roof'd Tortoises do dwell
In cases fit of Tortoise-shell:
No Creature loves an empty space;   15
Their Bodies measure out their Place.

III

But He, superfluously spread,
Demands more room alive then dead.
And in his hollow Palace goes
Where Winds as he themselves may lose.   20
What need of all this Marble Crust
T'impark the wanton Mote of Dust,
That thinks by Breadth the World t'unite
Though the first Builders fail'd in Height?

IV

But all things are composed here   25
Like Nature, orderly and near:
In which we the Dimensions find
Of that more sober Age and Mind,
When larger sized Men did stoop
To enter at a narrow loop;   30
As practising, in doors so strait,
To strain themselves through *Heavens Gate.*

V

And surely when the after Age
Shall hither come in *Pilgrimage,*
These sacred Places to adore,   35
By *Vere* and *Fairfax* trod before,
Men will dispute how their Extent
Within such dwarfish Confines went:
And some will smile at this, as well
As *Romulus* his Bee-like Cell.   40

VI

Humility alone designs
Those short but admirable Lines,
By which, ungirt and unconstrain'd,
Things greater are in less contain'd.
Let others vainly strive t'immure   45
The *Circle* in the *Quadrature*!
These *holy Mathematicks* can
In ev'ry Figure equal Man.

VII

Yet thus the laden House does sweat,
And scarce indures the *Master* great: 50
But where he comes the swelling Hall
Stirs, and the *Square* grows *Spherical*;
More by his *Magnitude* distrest,
Then he is by its straitness prest:
And too officiously it slights   55
That in it self which him delights.

VIII

So Honour better Lowness bears,
Then That unwonted Greatness wears.
Height with a certain Grace does bend,
But low Things clownishly ascend.   60
And yet what needs there here Excuse,
Where ev'ry Thing does answer Use?
Where neatness nothing can condemn,
Nor Pride invent what to contemn?

IX

A Stately *Frontispice of Poor*   65
Adorns without the open Door:
Nor less the Rooms within commends
Daily new *Furniture of Friends*.

The House was built upon the Place
Only as for *a Mark of Grace*;   70
And for an *Inn* to entertain
Its *Lord* a while, but not remain.

X

Him *Bishops-Hill*, or *Denton* may,
Or *Bilbrough*, better hold then they:
But Nature here hath been so free   75
As if she said leave this to me.
Art would more neatly have defac'd
What she had laid so sweetly wast;
In fragrant Gardens, shady Woods,
Deep Meadows, and transparent Floods.   80

XI

While with slow Eyes we these survey,
And on each pleasant footstep stay,
We opportunly may relate
The Progress of this Houses Fate.
A *Nunnery* first gave it birth.   85
For *Virgin Buildings* oft brought forth.
And all that Neighbour-Ruine shows
The Quarries whence this dwelling rose.

XII

Near to this gloomy Cloysters Gates
There dwelt the blooming Virgin *Thwates*;   90
Fair beyond Measure, and an Heir
Which might Deformity make fair.
And oft She spent the Summer Suns
Discoursing with the *Suttle Nunns*.
Whence in these Words one to her weav'd,   95
(As 'twere by Chance) Thoughts long conceiv'd.

XIII

'Within this holy leisure we
'Live innocently as you see.
'These Walls restrain the World without,
'But hedge our Liberty about.   100
'These Bars inclose that wider Den
'Of those wild Creatures, called Men.
'The Cloyster outward shuts its Gates,
'And, from us, locks on them the Grates.

XIV

'Here we, in shining Armour white,   105
'Like *Virgin Amazons* do fight.
'And our chast *Lamps* we hourly trim,
'Lest the great *Bridegroom* find them dim.
'Our *Orient* Breaths perfumed are
'With insense of incessant Pray'r.   110
'And Holy-water of our Tears
'Most strangly our Complexion clears.

XV

'Not Tears of Grief; but such as those
'With which calm Pleasure overflows;
'Or Pity, when we look on you   115
'That live without this happy Vow.
'How should we grieve that must be seen
'Each one a *Spouse*, and each a *Queen*;
'And can in *Heaven* hence behold
'Our brighter Robes and Crowns of Gold?   120

XVI

'When we have prayed all our Beads,
'Some One the holy *Legend* reads;
'While all the rest with Needles paint
'The Face and Graces of the *Saint*.

'But what the Linnen can't receive   125
'They in their Lives do interweave.
'This Work the *Saints* best represents;
'That serves for *Altar's Ornaments*.

XVII

'But much it to our work would add
'If here your hand, your Face we had: 130
'By it we would *our Lady* touch;
'Yet thus She you resembles much.
'Some of your Features, as we sow'd,
'Through ev'ry *Shrine* should be bestow'd.
'And in one Beauty we would take   135
'Enough a thousand *Saints* to make.

XVIII

'And (for I dare not quench the Fire
'That me does for your good inspire)
''Twere Sacriledge a Man t'admit
'To holy things, for *Heaven* fit.   140
'I see the *Angels* in a Crown
'On you the Lillies show'ring down:
'And round about you Glory breaks,
'That something more then humane speaks.

XIX

'All Beauty, when at such a height,   145
'Is so already consecrate.
'*Fairfax* I know; and long ere this
'Have mark'd the Youth, and what he is.
'But can he such a *Rival* seem
'For whom you *Heav'n* should disesteem?   150
'Ah, no! and 'twould more Honour prove
'He your *Devoto* were, then *Love*.

XX

'Here live beloved, and obey'd:
'Each one your Sister, each your Maid.
'And, if our Rule seem strictly pend,　　　**155**
'The Rule it self to you shall bend.
'Our *Abbess* too, now far in Age,
'Doth your succession near presage.
'How soft the yoke on us would lye,
'Might such fair Hands as yours it tye!　　　**160**

XXI

'Your voice, the sweetest of the Quire,
'Shall draw *Heav'n* nearer, raise us higher.
'And your Example, if our Head,
'Will soon us to perfection lead.
'Those Virtues to us all so dear,　　　**165**
'Will straight grow Sanctity when here:
'And that, once sprung, increase so fast
'Till Miracles it work at last.

XXII

'Nor is our *Order* yet so nice,
'Delight to banish as a Vice.　　　**170**
'Here Pleasure Piety doth meet;
'One perfecting the other Sweet.
'So through the mortal fruit we boyl
'The Sugars uncorrupting Oyl:
'And that which perisht while we pull,　　　**175**
'Is thus preserved clear and full.

XXIII

'For such indeed are all our Arts;
'Still handling Natures finest Parts.
'Flow'rs dress the Altars; for the Clothes,
'The Sea-born Amber we compose;　　　**180**

'Balms for the griv'd we draw; and Pasts
'We mold, as Baits for curious tasts.
'What need is here of Man? unless
'These as sweet Sins we should confess.

XXIV

'Each Night among us to your side   185
'Appoint a fresh and Virgin Bride;
'Whom if *our Lord* at midnight find,
'Yet Neither should be left behind.
'Where you may lye as chast in Bed,
'As Pearls together billeted.   190
'All Night embracing Arm in Arm,
'Like Chrystal pure with Cotton warm.

XXV

'But what is this to all the store
'Of Joys you see, and may make more!
'Try but a while, if you be wise: 195
'The Tryal neither Costs, nor Tyes.
Now *Fairfax* seek her promis'd faith:
Religion that dispensed hath;
Which She hence forward does begin;
The *Nuns* smooth Tongue has suckt her in.   200

XXVI

Oft, though he knew it was in vain,
Yet would he valiantly complain.
'Is this that *Sanctity* so great,
'An Art by which you finly'r cheat?
'Hypocrite Witches, hence *avant*,   205
'Who though in prison yet inchant!
'Death only can such Theeves make fast,
'As rob though in the Dungeon cast.

XXVII

'Were there but, when this House was made,
'One Stone that a just Hand had laid,   210
'It must have fall'n upon her Head
'Who first Thee from thy Faith misled.
'And yet, how well soever ment,
'With them 'twould soon grow fraudulent:
'For like themselves they alter all,   215
'And vice infects the very Wall.

XXVIII

'But sure those Buildings last not long,
'Founded by Folly, kept by Wrong.
'I know what Fruit their Gardens yield,
'When they it think by Night conceal'd.   220
'Fly from their Vices. 'Tis thy state,
'Not Thee, that they would consecrate.
'Fly from their Ruine. How I fear
'Though guiltless lest thou perish there.'

XXIX

What should he do? He would respect   225
Religion, but not Right neglect:
For first Religion taught him Right,
And dazled not but clear'd his sight.
Sometimes resolv'd his Sword he draws,
But reverenceth then the Laws: 230
For Justice still that Courage led;
First from a Judge, then Souldier bred.

XXX

Small Honour would be in the Storm.
The *Court* him grants the lawful Form;
Which licens'd either Peace or Force,   235
To hinder the unjust Divorce.

Yet still the *Nuns* his Right debar'd,
Standing upon their holy Guard.
Ill-counsell'd Women, do you know
Whom you resist, or what you do?   240

XXXI

Is not this he whose Offspring fierce
Shall fight through all the *Universe*;
And with successive Valour try
France, *Poland*, either *Germany*;
Till one, as long since prophecy'd,   245
His Horse through conquer'd *Britain* ride?
Yet, against Fate, his Spouse they kept;
And the great Race would intercept.

XXXII

Some to the Breach against their Foes
Their *Wooden Saints* in vain oppose.   250
Another bolder stands at push
With their old *Holy-Water Brush*.
While the disjointed *Abbess* threads
The gingling Chain-shot of her *Beads*.
But their lowd'st Cannon were their Lungs;   255
And sharpest Weapons were their Tongues.

XXXIII

But, waving these aside like Flyes,
Young *Fairfax* through the Wall does rise,
Then th' unfrequented Vault appear'd,
And superstitions vainly fear'd.   260
The *Relicks false* were set to view;
Only the Jewels there were true.
But truly bright and holy *Thwaites*
That weeping at the *Altar* waites.

XXXIIII

But the glad Youth away her bears,   265
And to the *Nuns* bequeaths her Tears:
Who guiltily their Prize bemoan,
Like Gipsies that a Child hath stoln.
Thenceforth (as when th' Inchantment ends
The Castle vanishes or rends)   270
The wasting Cloister with the rest
Was in one instant dispossest.

XXXV

At the demolishing, this Seat
To *Fairfax* fell as by Escheat.
And what both *Nuns* and *Founders* will'd   275
'Tis likely better thus fulfill'd.
For if the *Virgin* prov'd not theirs,
The *Cloyster* yet remained hers.
Though many a *Nun* there made her Vow,
'Twas no *Religious House* till now.   280

XXXVI

From that blest Bed the *Heroe* came,
Whom *France* and *Poland* yet does fame:
Who, when retired here to Peace,
His warlike Studies could not cease;
But laid these Gardens out in sport   285
In the just Figure of a Fort;
And with five Bastions it did fence,
As aiming one for ev'ry Sense.

XXXVII

When in the *East* the Morning Ray
Hangs out the Colours of the Day,   290
The Bee through these known Allies hums,
Beating the *Dian* with its *Drumms*.

Then Flow'rs their drowsie Eylids raise,
Their Silken Ensigns each displayes,
And dries its Pan yet dank with Dew,   295
And fills its Flask with Odours new.

XXXVIII

These, as their *Governour* goes by,
In fragrant Vollyes they let fly;
And to salute their *Governess*
Again as great a charge they press: 300
None for the *Virgin Nymph*; for She
Seems with the Flow'rs a Flow'r to be.
And think so still! though not compare
With Breath so sweet, or Cheek so faire.

XXXIX

Well shot ye Firemen! Oh how sweet,   305
And round your equal Fires do meet;
Whose shrill report no Ear can tell,
But Ecchoes to the Eye and smell.
See how the Flow'rs, as at *Parade*,
Under their *Colours* stand displaid: 310
Each *Regiment* in order grows,
That of the Tulip Pinke and Rose.

XL

But when the vigilant *Patroul*
Of Stars walks round about the *Pole*,
Their Leaves, that to the stalks are curl'd,   315
Seem to their Staves the *Ensigns* furl'd.
Then in some Flow'rs beloved Hut
Each Bee as Sentinel is shut;
And sleeps so too: but, if once stir'd,
She runs you through, nor askes *the Word*.   320

XLI

Oh Thou, that dear and happy Isle
The Garden of the World ere while,
Thou *Paradise* of four Seas,
Which *Heaven* planted us to please,
But, to exclude the World, did guard   325
With watry if not flaming Sword;
What luckless Apple did we tast,
To make us Mortal, and The Wast?

XLII

Unhappy! shall we never more
That sweet *Militia* restore,   330
When Gardens only had their Towrs,
And all the Garrisons were Flowrs,
When Roses only Arms might bear,
And Men did rosie Garlands wear?
Tulips, in several Colours barr'd,   335
Were then the *Switzers* of our *Guard*.

XLIII

The *Gardiner* had the *Souldiers* place,
And his more gentle Forts did trace.
The Nursery of all things green
Was then the only *Magazeen*.   340
The *Winter Quarters* were the Stoves,
Where he the tender Plants removes.
But War all this doth overgrow:
We Ord'nance Plant and Powder sow.

XLIV

And yet there walks one on the Sod   345
Who, had it pleased him and *God*,
Might once have made our Gardens spring
Fresh as his own and flourishing.

But he preferr'd to the *Cinque Ports*
These five imaginary Forts: 350
And, in those half-dry Trenches, spann'd
Pow'r which the Ocean might command.

XLV

For he did, with his utmost Skill,
Ambition weed, but *Conscience* till.
Conscience, that Heaven-nursed Plant,   355
Which most our Earthly Gardens want.
A prickling leaf it bears, and such
As that which shrinks at ev'ry touch;
But Flowrs eternal, and divine,
That in the Crowns of Saints do shine.   360

XLVI

The sight does from these *Bastions* ply,
Th' invisible *Artilery*;
And at proud *Cawood Castle* seems
To point the *Battery* of its Beams.
As if it quarrell'd in the Seat   365
Th' Ambition of its *Prelate* great.
But ore the Meads below it plays,
Or innocently seems to gaze.

XLVII

And now to the Abbyss I pass
Of that unfathomable Grass,   370
Where Men like Grashoppers appear,
But Grashoppers are Gyants there:
They, in their squeking Laugh, contemn
Us as we walk more low then them:
And, from the Precipices tall   375
Of the green spir's, to us do call.

XLVIII

To see Men through this Meadow **Dive,**
We wonder how they rise alive.
As, under Water, none does know
Whether he fall through it or go.   380
But, as the Marriners that sound,
And show upon their Lead the Ground,
They bring up Flow'rs so to be seen,
And prove they've at the Bottom been.

XLIX

No Scene that turns with Engines strange   385
Does oftner then these Meadows change.
For when the Sun the Grass hath vext,
The tawny Mowers enter next;
Who seem like *Israelites* to be,
Walking on foot through a green Sea.   390
To them the Grassy Deeps divide,
And crowd a Lane to either Side.

L

With whistling Sithe, and Elbow strong,
These Massacre the Grass along:
While one, unknowing, carves the *Rail,*   395
Whose yet unfeather'd Quils her fail.
The Edge all bloody from its Breast
He draws, and does his stroke detest;
Fearing the Flesh untimely mow'd
To him a Fate as black forebode.   400

LI

But bloody *Thestylis,* that waites
To bring the mowing Camp their Cates,
Greedy as Kites has trust it up,
And forthwith means on it to sup:

When on another quick She lights, 405
And cryes, he call'd us *Israelites*;
But now, to make his saying true,
Rails rain for Quails, for Manna Dew.

LII

Unhappy Birds! what does it boot
To build below the Grasses Root; 410
When Lowness is unsafe as Hight,
And Chance o'retakes what scapeth spight?
And now your Orphan Parents Call
Sounds your untimely Funeral.
Death-Trumpets creak in such a Note, 415
And 'tis the *Sourdine* in their Throat.

LIII

Or sooner hatch or higher build:
The Mower now commands the Field;
In whose new Traverse seemeth wrought
A Camp of Battail newly fought: 420
Where, as the Meads with Hay, the Plain
Lyes quilted ore with Bodies slain:
The Women that with forks it fling,
Do represent the Pillaging.

LIV

And now the careless Victors play, 425
Dancing the Triumphs of the Hay;
Where every Mowers wholesome Heat
Smells like an *Alexanders sweat*.
Their Females fragrant as the Mead
Which they in *Fairy Circles* tread: 430
When at their Dances End they kiss,
Their new-made Hay not sweeter is.

LV

When after this 'tis pil'd in Cocks,
Like a calm Sea it shews the Rocks:
We wondring in the River near   435
How Boats among them safely steer.
Or, like the *Desert Memphis Sand*,
Short *Pyramids* of Hay do stand.
And such the *Roman Camps* do rise
In Hills for Soldiers Obsequies.   440

LVI

This *Scene* again withdrawing brings
A new and empty Face of things;
A levell'd space, as smooth and plain,
As Clothes for *Lilly* strecht to stain.
The World when first created sure   445
Was such a Table rase and pure.
Or rather such is the *Toril*
Ere the Bulls enter at Madril.

LVII

For to this naked equal Flat,
Which *Levellers* take Pattern at,   450
The Villagers in common chase
Their Cattle, which it closer rase;
And what below the Sith increast
Is pincht yet nearer by the Beast.
Such, in the painted World, appear'd   455
Davenant with th' Universal Heard.

LVIII

They seem within the polisht Grass
A Landskip drawen in Looking-Glass.
And shrunk in the huge Pasture show
As Spots, so shap'd, on Faces do.   460

Such Fleas, ere they approach the Eye,
In Multiplying Glasses lye.
They feed so wide, so slowly move,
As *Constellations* do above.

LIX

Then, to conclude these pleasant Acts,   465
Denton sets ope its *Cataracts*;
And makes the Meadow truly be
(What it but seem'd before) a Sea.
For, jealous of its *Lords* long stay,
It try's t'invite him thus away.   470
The River in it self is drown'd,
And Isl's th' astonish'd Cattle round.

LX

Let others tell the *Paradox*,
How Eels now bellow in the Ox;
How Horses at their Tails do kick,   475
Turn'd as they hang to Leeches quick;
How Boats can over Bridges sail;
And Fishes do the Stables scale.
How *Salmons* trespassing are found;
And Pikes are taken in the Pound.   480

LXI

But I, retiring from the Flood,
Take Sanctuary in the Wood;
And, while it lasts, my self imbark
In this yet green, yet growing Ark;
Where the first Carpenter might best   485
Fit Timber for his Keel have Prest.
And where all Creatures might have shares,
Although in Armies, not in Paires.

LXII

The double Wood of ancient Stocks
Link'd in so thick, an Union locks,   490
It like two *Pedigrees* appears,
On one hand *Fairfax*, th' other *Veres*:
Of whom though many fell in War,
Yet more to Heaven shooting are:
And, as they Natures Cradle deckt,   495
Will in green Age her Hearse expect.

LXIII

When first the Eye this Forrest sees
It seems indeed as *Wood* not *Trees*:
As if their Neighbourhood so old
To one great Trunk them all did mold.   500
There the huge Bulk takes place, as ment
To thrust up a *Fifth Element*;
And stretches still so closely wedg'd
As if the Night within were hedg'd.

LXIV

Dark all without it knits; within   505
It opens passable and thin;
And in as loose an order grows,
As the *Corinthean Porticoes*.
The arching Boughs unite between
The Columnes of the Temple green;   510
And underneath the winged Quires
Echo about their tuned Fires.

LXV

The *Nightingale* does here make choice
To sing the Tryals of her Voice.
Low Shrubs she sits in, and adorns   515
With Musick high the squatted Thorns.

E

But highest Oakes stoop down to hear,
And listning Elders prick the Ear.
The Thorn, lest it should hurt her, draws
Within the Skin its shrunken claws.   520

LXVI

But I have for my Musick found
A Sadder, yet more pleasing Sound:
The *Stock-doves*, whose fair necks are grac'd
With Nuptial Rings their Ensigns chast;
Yet always, for some Cause unknown,   525
Sad pair unto the Elms they moan.
O why should such a Couple mourn,
That in so equal Flames do burn!

LXVII

Then as I careless on the Bed
Of gelid *Straw-berryes* do tread,   530
And through the Hazles thick espy
The hatching *Thrastles* shining Eye;
The *Heron* from the Ashes top,
The eldest of its young lets drop,
As if it Stork-like did pretend   535
That *Tribute* to *its Lord* to send.

LXVIII

But most the *Hewel's* wonders are,
Who here has the *Holt-felsters* care.
He walks still upright from the Root,
Meas'ring the Timber with his Foot;   540
And all the way, to keep it clean,
Doth from the Bark the Wood-moths glean.
He, with his Beak, examines well
Which fit to stand and which to fell.

LXIX

The good he numbers up, and hacks;   545
As if he mark'd them with the Ax.
But where he, tinkling with his Beak,
Does find the hollow Oak to speak,
That for his building he designs,
And through the tainted Side he mines.   550
Who could have thought the *tallest Oak*
Should fall by such a *feeble Strok*'!

LXX

Nor would it, had the Tree not fed
A *Traitor-worm*, within it bred.
(As first our *Flesh* corrupt within   555
Tempts impotent and bashful *Sin*.
And yet that *Worm* triumphs not long,
But serves to feed the *Hewels young*.
While the Oake seems to fall content,
Viewing the Treason's Punishment.   560

LXXI

Thus I, *easie Philosopher*,
Among the *Birds* and *Trees* confer:
And little now to make me, wants
Or of the *Fowles*, or of the *Plants*.
Give me but Wings as they, and I   565
Streight floting on the Air shall fly:
Or turn me but, and you shall see
I was but an inverted Tree.

LXXII

Already I begin to call
In their most learned Original: 570
And where I Language want, my Signs
The Bird upon the Bough divines;

And more attentive there doth sit
Then if She were with Lime-twigs knit.
No Leaf does tremble in the Wind   575
Which I returning cannot find.

LXXIII

Out of these scatter'd *Sibyls* Leaves
Strange *Prophecies* my Phancy weaves:
And in one History consumes,
Like *Mexique Paintings*, all the *Plumes*.   580
What *Rome*, *Greece*, *Palestine*, ere said
I in this light *Mosaick* read.
Thrice happy he who, not mistook,
Hath read in *Natures mystick Book*.

LXXIV

And see how Chance's better Wit   585
Could with a Mask my studies hit!
The Oak-Leaves me embroyder all,
Between which Caterpillars crawl:
And Ivy, with familiar trails,
Me licks, and clasps, and curles, and hales.   590
Under this *antick Cope* I move
Like some great *Prelate of the Grove*,

LXXV

Then, languishing with ease, I toss
On Pallets swoln of Velvet Moss;
While the Wind, cooling through the Boughs,
Flatters with Air my panting Brows.   596
Thanks for my Rest ye *Mossy Banks*,
And unto you *cool Zephyr's* Thanks,
Who, as my Hair, my Thoughts too shed,
And winnow from the Chaff my Head.   600

LXXVI

How safe, methinks, and strong, behind
These Trees have I incamp'd my Mind;
Where Beauty, aiming at the Heart,
Bends in some Tree its useless Dart;
And where the World no certain Shot   605
Can make, or me it toucheth not.
But I on it securely play,
And gaul its Horsemen all the Day.

LXXVII

Bind me ye *Woodbines* in your 'twines,
Curle me about ye gadding *Vines*,   610
And Oh so close your Circles lace,
That I may never leave this Place:
But, lest your Fetters prove too weak,
Ere I your Silken Bondage break,
Do you, *O Brambles*, chain me too,   615
And courteous *Briars* nail me through.

LXXVIII

Here in the Morning tye my Chain,
Where the two Woods have made a Lane:
While, like a *Guard* on either side,
The Trees before their *Lord* divide;   620
This, like a long and equal Thread,
Betwixt two *Labyrinths* does lead.
But, where the Floods did lately drown,
There at the Ev'ning stake me down.

LXXIX

For now the Waves are fal'n and dry'd,   625
And now the Meadows fresher dy'd;
Whose Grass, with moister colour dasht,
Seems as green Silks but newly washt.

No *Serpent* new nor *Crocodile*
Remains behind our little *Nile*;   630
Unless it self you will mistake,
Among these Meads the only Snake.

LXXX

See in what wanton harmless folds
It ev'ry where the Meadow holds;
And its yet muddy back doth lick,   635
Till as a *Chrystal Mirrour* slick;
Where all things gaze themselves, and doubt
If they be in it or without.
And for his shade which therein shines,
Narcissus like, the *Sun* too pines.   640

LXXXI

Oh what a Pleasure 'tis to hedge
My Temples here with heavy sedge;
Abandoning my lazy Side,
Stretcht as a Bank unto the Tide;
Or to suspend my sliding Foot   645
On the Osiers undermined Root,
And in its Branches tough to hang,
While at my Lines the Fishes twang!

LXXXII

But now away my Hooks, my Quills,
And Angles, idle Utensils.   650
The *young Maria* walks to night:
Hide trifling Youth thy Pleasures slight.
'Twere shame that such judicious Eyes
Should with such Toyes a Man surprize;
She that already is the *Law*   655
Of all her *Sex*, her *Ages Aw*.

LXXXIII

See how loose Nature, in respect
To her, it self doth recollect;
And every thing so whisht and fine,
Starts forth with to its *Bonne Mine*.   660
The *Sun* himself, of *Her* aware,
Seems to descend with greater Care;
And lest *She* see him go to Bed,
In blushing Clouds conceales his Head.

LXXXIV

So when the Shadows laid asleep   665
From underneath these Banks do creep,
And on the River as it flows
With *Eben Shuts* begin to close;
The modest *Halcyon* comes in sight,
Flying betwixt the Day and Night;   670
And such an horror calm and dumb,
Admiring Nature does benum.

LXXXV

The viscous Air, wheres'ere She fly,
Follows and sucks her Azure dy;
The gellying Stream compacts below,   675
If it might fix her shadow so;
The stupid Fishes hang, as plain
As *Flies* in *Chrystal* overt'ane;
And Men the silent *Scene* assist,
Charm'd with the *Saphir-winged Mist*.   680

LXXXVI

Maria such, and so doth hush
The *World*, and through the *Ev'ning* rush.
No new-born *Comet* such a Train
Draws through the Skie, nor Star new-slain.

For streight those giddy Rockets fail,   685
Which from the putrid Earth exhale,
But by her *Flames*, in *Heaven* try'd,
Nature is wholly *vitrifi'd*.

LXXXVII

'Tis *She* that to these Gardens gave
That wondrous Beauty which they have;   690
She streightness on the Woods bestows;
To *Her* the Meadow sweetness owes;
Nothing could make the River be
So Chrystal-pure but only *She*;
She yet more Pure, Sweet, Streight, and Fair, 695
Then Gardens, Woods, Meads, Rivers are.

LXXXVIII

Therefore what first *She* on them spent,
They gratefully again present.
The Meadow Carpets where to tread;
The Garden Flow'rs to Crown *Her* Head;   700
And for a Glass the limpid Brook,
Where *She* may all *her* Beautyes look;
But, since *She* would not have them seen,
The Wood about *her* draws a Skreen.

LXXXIX

For *She*, to higher Beauties rais'd,   705
Disdains to be for lesser prais'd.
She counts her Beauty to converse
In all the Languages as *hers*;
Nor yet in those *her self* imployes
But for the *Wisdome*, not the *Noyse*;   710
Nor yet that *Wisdome* would affect,
But as 'tis *Heavens Dialect*.

LXXXX

Blest *Nymph*! that couldst so soon prevent
Those *Trains* by Youth against thee meant;
Tears (watry Shot that pierce the Mind;)   715
And *Sighs* (Loves Cannon charg'd with Wind;)
True Praise (That breaks through all defence;)
And *feign'd complying Innocence*;
But knowing where this *Ambush* lay,
She scap'd the safe, but roughest Way.   720

LXXXXI

This 'tis to have been from the first
In a *Domestick Heaven* nurst,
Under the *Discipline* severe
Of *Fairfax* and the starry *Vere*;
Where not one object can come nigh   725
But pure, and spotless as the Eye;
And *Goodness* doth it self intail
On *Females*, if there want a *Male*.

LXXXXII

Go now fond Sex that on your Face
Do all your useless Study place,   730
Nor once at Vice your Brows dare knit
Lest the smooth Forehead wrinkled sit:
Yet your own Face shall at you grin,
Thorough the Black-bag of your Skin;
When *knowledge* only could have fill'd   735
And *Virtue* all those *Furrows till'd*.

LXXXXIII

Hence *She* with Graces more divine
Supplies beyond her *Sex* the *Line*;
And, like a *sprig of Misleto*,
On the *Fairfacian Oak* does grow;   740

Whence, for some universal good,
The *Priest* shall cut the sacred Bud;
While her *glad Parents* most rejoice,
And make their *Destiny* their *Choice.*

LXXXXIV

Mean time ye Fields, Springs, Bushes, Flow'rs,
Where yet She leads her studious Hours,   746
(Till Fate her worthily translates,
And find a *Fairfax* for our *Thwaites*)
Employ the means you have by Her,
And in your kind your selves preferr;   750
That, as all *Virgins* She preceds,
So you all *Woods, Streams, Gardens, Meads.*

LXXXXV

For you *Thessalian Tempe's Seat*
Shall now be scorn'd as obsolete;
Aranjuez, as less, disdain'd;   755
The *Bel-Retiro* as constrain'd;
But name not the *Idalian Grove*,
For 'twas the Seat of wanton Love;
Much less the Dead's *Elysian Fields,*
Yet nor to them your Beauty yields.   760

LXXXXVI

'Tis not, what once it was, the *World*:
But a rude heap together hurl'd;
All negligently overthrown,
Gulfes, Deserts, Precipices, Stone.
Your lesser *World* contains the same.   765
But in more decent Order tame;
You Heaven's Center, Nature's Lap.
And Paradice's only Map.

LXXXXVII

But now the *Salmon-Fisher's* moist
Their *Leathern Boats* begin to hoist;   770
And, like *Antipodes* in Shoes,
Have shod their *Heads* in their *Canoos.*
How *Tortoise* like, but not so slow,
These rational *Amphibii* go?
Let's in: for the dark *Hemisphere*   775
Does now like one of them appear.

*On the Victory obtained by Blake
over the Spaniards
in the Bay of Sanctacruze,
in the Island of Teneriff, 1657*

Now does *Spains* Fleet her spatious wings unfold,
Leaves the new World and hastens for the old:
But though the wind was fair, they slowly swoome
Frayted with acted Guilt, and Guilt to come:
For this rich load, of which so proud they are,   5
Was rais'd by Tyranny, and rais'd for War;
Every capatious Gallions womb was fill'd,
With what the Womb of wealthy Kingdomes yield,
The new Worlds wounded Intrails they had tore,
For wealth wherewith to wound the old once more.
Wealth which all others Avarice might cloy,   11
But yet in them caus'd as much fear, as Joy.
For now upon the Main, themselves they saw,
That boundless Empire, where you give the Law,
Of winds and waters rage, they fearful be,   15
But much more fearful are your Flags to see.
Day, that to those who sail upon the deep,
More wish't for, and more welcome is then sleep,

They dreaded to behold, Least the Sun's light,
With *English* Streamers, should salute their sight: 20
In thickest darkness they would choose to steer,
So that such darkness might suppress their fear;
At length theirs vanishes, and fortune smiles;
For they behold the sweet Canary Isles;
One of which doubtless is by Nature blest   25
Above both Worlds, since 'tis above the rest.
For least some Gloominess might stain her sky,
Trees there the duty of the Clouds supply;
O noble Trust which Heaven on this Isle poures,
Fertile to be, yet never need her showres.   30
A happy People, which at once do gain
The benefits without the ills of rain.
Both health and profit Fate cannot deny;
Where still the Earth is moist, the Air still dry;
The jarring Elements no discord know,   35
Fewel and Rain together kindly grow;
And coolness there, with heat doth never fight,
This only rules by day, and that by Night.
Your worth to all these Isles, a just right brings,
The best of Lands should have the best of Kings.   40
And these want nothing Heaven can afford,
Unless it be, the having you their Lord;
But this great want, will not a long one prove,
Your Conquering Sword will soon that want remove.
For *Spain* had better, Shee'l ere long confess,   45
Have broken all her Swords, then this one Peace,
Casting that League off, which she held so long,
She cast off that which only made her strong.
Forces and art, she soon will feel, are vain,
Peace, against you, was the sole strength of *Spain*. 50
By that alone those Islands she secures,
Peace made them hers, but War will make them yours
There the indulgent Soil that rich Grape breeds,
Which of the Gods the fancied drink exceeds;

They still do yield, such is their pretious mould, 55
All that is good, and are not curst with Gold.
With fatal Gold, for still where that does grow,
Neither the Soyl, nor People quiet know.
Which troubles men to raise it when 'tis ore,
And when 'tis raised, does trouble them much more.
Ah, why was thither brought that cause of War, 61
Kind Nature had from thence remov'd so far.
In vain doth she those Islands free from Ill,
If fortune can make guilty what she will.
But whilst I draw that Scene, where you ere long, 65
Shall conquests act, your present are unsung,

    For *Sanctacruze* the glad Fleet takes her way.
And safely there casts Anchor in the Bay.
Never so many with one joyful cry,
That place saluted, where they all must dye. 70
Deluded men! Fate with you did but sport,
You scap't the Sea, to perish in your Port.
'Twas more for *Englands* fame you should dye there,
Where you had most of strength, and least of fear.

    The Peek's proud height, the *Spaniards* all admire,
Yet in their brests, carry a pride much higher. 76
Onely to this vast hill a power is given,
At once both to Inhabit Earth and Heaven.
But this stupendious Prospect did not neer,
Make them admire, so much as they did fear. 80

    For here they met with news, which did produce,
A grief, above the cure of Grapes best juice.
They learn'd with Terrour, that nor Summers heat,
Nor Winters storms, had made your Fleet retreat.
To fight against such Foes, was vain they knew, 85
Which did the rage of Elements subdue.
Who on the Ocean that does horror give,
To all besides, triumphantly do live.

    With hast they therefore all their Gallions moar,
And flank with Cannon from the Neighbouring shore.

109

Forts, Lines, and Sconces all the Bay along,   91
They build and act all that can make them strong.
    Fond men who know not whilst such works they
      raise,
They only Labour to exalt your praise.
Yet they by restless toyl, became at Length,   95
So proud and confident of their made strength.
That they with joy their boasting General heard,
Wish then for that assault he lately fear'd.
His wish he has, for now undaunted *Blake*,
With winged speed, for *Sanctacruze* does make.   100
For your renown, his conquering Fleet does ride,
Ore Seas as vast as is the *Spaniards* pride.
Whose Fleet and Trenches view'd, he soon did say,
We to their Strength are more obilg'd then they.
Were't not for that, they from their Fate would run,
And a third World seek out our Armes to shun.   106
Those Forts, which there, so high and strong appear.
Do not so much suppress, as shew their fear.
Of Speedy Victory let no man doubt,
Our worst works past, now we have found them out.
Behold their Navy does at Anchor lye,   111
And they are ours, for now they cannot fly.
    This said, the whole Fleet gave it their applause,
And all assumes your courage, in your cause.
That Bay they enter, which unto them owes,   115
The noblest wreaths, that Victory bestows.
Bold *Stainer* Leads, this Fleets design'd by fate.
To give him Lawrel, as the Last did Plate.
    The Thund'ring Cannon now begins the Fight,
And though it be at Noon, creates a Night.   120
The Air was soon after the fight begun,
Far more enflam'd by it, then by the Sun.
Never so burning was that Climate known,
War turn'd the temperate, to the Torrid Zone.
    Fate these two Fleets, between both Worlds had
      brought   125

Who fight, as if for both those Worlds they fought.
Thousands of wayes, Thousands of men there dye,
Some Ships are sunk, some blown up in the skie.
Nature ne'r made Cedars so high aspire,
As Oakes did then, Urg'd by the active fire.   130
Which by quick powders force, so high was sent,
That it return'd to its own Element.
Torn Limbs some leagues into the Island fly,
Whilst others lower, in the Sea do lye.
Scarce souls from bodies sever'd are so far,   135
By death, as bodies there were by the War.
Th' all-seeing Sun, neer gaz'd on such a sight,
Two dreadful Navies there at Anchor Fight.
And neither have, or power, or will to fly,
There one must Conquer, or there both must dye. 140
Far different Motives yet, engag'd them thus,
Necessity did them, but Choice did us.

    A choice which did the highest worth express,
And was attended by as high success.
For your resistless genious there did Raign,   145
By which we Laurels reapt ev'n on the Mayn.
So prosperous Stars, though absent to the sence,
Bless those they shine for, by their Influence.

    Our Cannon now tears every Ship and Sconce,
And o're two Elements Triumphs at once.   150
Their Gallions sunk, their wealth the Sea does fill,
The only place where it can cause no Ill.

    Ah would those Treasures which both Indies have,
Were buryed in as large, and deep a grave,
Wars chief support with them would buried be,   155
And the Land owe her peace unto the Sea.
Ages to come, your conquering Arms will bless,
There they destroy, what had destroy'd their Peace.
And in one War the present age may boast,
That certain seeds of many Wars are lost.   160

    All the Foes Ships destroy'd, by Sea or fire,
Victorious *Blake*, does from the Bay retire,

His Seige of *Spain* he then again pursues,
And there first brings of his success the news;
The saddest news that ere to *Spain* was brought,   165
Their rich Fleet sunk, and ours with Lawrel fraught.
Whilst fame in every place, her Trumpet blowes,
And tells the World, how much to you it owes.

A Dialogue between Thyrsis and Dorinda

Dorinda. WHEN Death, shall part us from these Kids,
            And shut up our divided Lids,
            Tell me, *Thyrsis*, prethee do,
            Whither thou and I must go.

Thyrsis. To the Elizium: (*Dorinda*) oh where i'st?   5
Thyrsis. A Chast Soul, can never mis't.
Dorinda. I know no way, but one, our home;
            Is our cell Elizium?

Thyrsis. Turn thine Eye to yonder Skie,
            There the milky way doth lye;   10
            'Tis a sure but rugged way,
            That leads to Everlasting day.

Dorinda. There Birds may nest, but how can I,
            That have no wings and cannot fly?

Thyrsis. Do not sigh (fair Nimph) for fire   15
            Hath no wings, yet doth aspire
            Till it hit, against the pole,
            Heaven's the Centre of the Soul.

Dorinda. But in Elizium how do they
            Pass Eternity away?   20

Thyrsis. Oh, ther's, neither hope nor fear
   Ther's no Wolf, no Fox, nor Bear.
   No need of Dog to fetch our stray,
   Our Lightfoot we may give away;
   No Oat-pipe's needfull, there thine Ears 25
   May feast with Musick of the Spheres.

Dorinda. Oh sweet! oh sweet! How I my future state
   By silent thinking, Antidate:
   I prethee let us spend our time to come,
   In talking of *Elizium.*   30

Thyrsis. Then I'le go on: There, sheep are full
   Of sweetest grass, and softest wooll;
   There, birds sing Consorts, garlands grow,
   Cool winds do whisper, springs do flow.
   There, alwayes is, a rising Sun, 35
   And day is ever, but begun.
   Shepheards there, bear equal sway,
   And every Nimph's a Queen of *May.*

Dorinda. Ah me, ah me. *Thyrsis. Dorinda*, why do'st
   Cry?

Dorinda. I'm sick, I'm sick, and fain would dye: 40
   Convinc' me now, that this is true;
   By bidding, with mee, all adieu.

Thyrsis. I cannot live, without thee, I
   Will for thee, much more with thee dye.

Dorinda. Then let us give *Carillo* charge o'th Sheep, 45
   And thou and I'le pick poppies and them
    steep
   In wine, and drink on't even till we weep,
   So shall we smoothly pass away in sleep.

The Character of Holland

HOLLAND, that scarce deserves the name of *Land*,
As but th' Off-scouring of the *British Sand*;
And so much Earth as was contributed
By *English Pilots* when they heav'd the Lead;
Or what by th' Oceans slow alluvion fell,   5
Of shipwrackt Cockle and the Muscle-shell;
This indigested vomit of the Sea
Fell to the *Dutch* by just Propriety.

Glad then, as Miners that have found the Oar,
They with mad labour fish'd the *Land* to *Shoar*;   10
And div'd as desperately for each piece
Of Earth, as if't had been of *Ambergreece*;
Collecting anxiously small Loads of Clay,
Less then what building Swallows bear away;
Or then those Pills which sordid Beetles roul,   15
Tranfusing into them their Dunghil Soul.

How did they rivet, with Gigantick Piles,
Thorough the Center their new-catched Miles;
And to the stake a strugling Country bound,
Where barking Waves still bait the forced Ground;   20
Building their *watry Babel* far more high
To reach the *Sea*, then those to scale the *Sky*.

Yet still his claim the Injur'd Ocean laid,
And oft at Leap-frog ore their Steeples plaid:
As if on purpose it on Land had come   25
To shew them what's their *Mare Liberum*.
A daily deluge over them does boyl;
The Earth and Water play at *Level-coyl*;
The Fish oft-times the Burger dispossest,
And sat not as a Meat but as a Guest;   30
And oft the *Tritons* and the *Sea-Nymphs* saw
Whole sholes of *Dutch* serv'd up for *Cabillan*;
Or as they over the new Level rang'd
For pickled *Herring*, pickled *Heeren* chang'd.

Nature, it seem'd, asham'd of her mistake,   35
Would throw their Land away at *Duck* and *Drake*.
   Therefore *Necessity*, that first made *Kings*,
Something like *Government* among them brings.
For as with *Pygmees* who best kills the *Crane*,
Among the *hungry* he that treasures *Grain*,   40
Among the *blind* the one-ey'd *blinkard* reigns,
So rules among the *drowned* he that *draines*.
Not who first see the *rising Sun* commands,
But who could first discern the *rising Lands*.
Who best could know to pump an Earth so leak   45
Him they their *Lord* and *Country's Father* speak.
To make a *Bank* was a great *Plot of State*;
Invent a *Shov'l* and be a *Magistrate*.
Hence some small *Dyke-grave* unperceiv'd invades
The *Pow'r*, and grows as 'twere a *King of Spades*.   50
But for less envy some *joynt States* endures,
Who look like a *Commission of the Sewers*.
For these *Half-anders*, half wet, and half dry,
Nor bear *strict service*, nor *pure Liberty*.
   'Tis probable *Religion* after this   55
Came next in order; which they could not miss.
How could the *Dutch* but he converted, when
Th' *Apostles* were so many Fishermen?
Besides the Waters of themselves did rise,
And, as their Land, so them did re-baptize.   60
Though *Herring* for their *God* few voices mist,
And *Poor-John* to have been th' *Evangelist*.
Faith, that could never Twins conceive before,
Never so fertile, spawn'd upon this shore:
More pregnant then their *Marg'ret*, that laid down
For *Hans-in-Kelder* of a whole *Hans-Town*.   66
   Sure when *Religion* did it self imbark,
And from the *East* would *Westward* steer its Ark,
It struck, and splitting on this unknown ground,
Each one thence pillag'd the first piece he found: 70

Hence *Amsterdam*, *Turk-Christian-Pagan-Jew*,
Staple of Sects and Mint of Schisme grew;
That *Bank of Conscience*, where not one so strange
Opinion but finds Credit, and Exchange.
In vain for *Catholicks* our selves we bear;   **75**
The *universal Church* is onely there.
Nor can Civility there want for *Tillage*,
Where wisely for their *Court* they chose a *Village*.
How fit a Title clothes their *Governours*,
Themselves the *Hogs* as all their Subjects *Bores*!   **80**
    Let it suffice to give their Country Fame
That it had one *Civilis* call'd by Name,
Some Fifteen hundred and more years ago;
But surely never any that was so.
    See but their *Mairmaids* with their *Tails of Fish*, **85**
Reeking at *Church* over the *Chafing-Dish*.
A vestal Turf enshrin'd in Earthen Ware
Fumes through the loop-holes of a wooden Square.
Each to the *Temple* with these *Altars* tend,
But still does place it at her *Western End*:   **90**
While the fat steam of *Female Sacrifice*
Fills the *Priests Nostrils* and puts out his *Eyes*.
    Or what a Spectacle the *Skipper gross*,
A *Water-Hercules Butter-Coloss*,
Tunn'd up with all their sev'ral *Towns of Beer*;   **95**
When Stagg'ring upon some Land, *Snick and Sneer*,
They try, like Statuaries, if they can,
Cut out each others *Athos* to a Man:
And carve in their large Bodies, where they please,
The Armes of the *United Provinces*.   **100**
    But when such Amity at home is show'd;
What then are their confederacies abroad?
Let this one court'sie witness all the rest;
When their whole Navy they together prest,
Not Christian Captives to redeem from Bands: **105**
Or intercept the Western golden Sands:

No, but all ancient Rights and Leagues must vail.
Rather then to the *English* strike their sail;
To whom their weather-beaten *Province* ows
It self, when as some greater Vessel tows   110
A Cock-boat tost with the same wind and fate;
We buoy'd so often up their *sinking State.*

    Was this *Jus Belli & Pacis;* could this be
Cause why their *Burgomaster of the Sea*
Ram'd with Gun-powder, flaming with Brand wine,
Should raging hold his Linstock to the Mine?   116
While, with feign'd *Treaties,* they invade by stealth
Our sore new circumcised *Common wealth.*

    Yet of his vain Attempt no more he sees
Then of *Case-Butter* shot and *Bullet-Cheese.*   120
And the torn Navy stagger'd with him home,
While the Sea laught it self into a foam,
'Tis true since that (as fortune kindly sports,)
A wholesome Danger drove us to our Ports.
While half their banish'd keels the Tempest tost, 125
Half bound at home in Prison to the frost:
That ours mean time at leizure might careen,
In a calm Winter, under Skies Serene.
As the obsequious Air and Waters rest,
Till the dear *Halcyon* hatch out all its nest.   130
The *Common wealth* doth by its losses grow;
And, like its own Seas, only Ebbs to flow.
Besides that very Agitation laves,
And purges out the corruptible waves.

    And now again our armed *Bucentore*   135
Doth yearly their *Sea-Nuptials* restore.
And now the *Hydra of seaven Provinces*
Is strangled by our *Infant Hercules.*
Their Tortoise wants its vainly stretched neck;
Their Navy all our Conquest or our Wreck: 140
Or, what is left, their *Carthage* overcome
Would render fain unto our better *Rome.*

117

Unless our *Senate*, lest their Youth disuse,
The War, (but who would) Peace if begg'd refuse.
  For now of nothing may our *State* despair,   145
Darling of Heaven, and of Men the Care;
Provided that they be what they have been,
Watchful abroad, and honest still within.
For while our *Neptune* doth a *Trident* shake,
Steel'd with those piercing Heads, *Dean, Monck* and
    Blake.   150
And while *Jove* governs in the highest Sphere,
Vainly in *Hell* let *Pluto* domineer.

An Horatian Ode
upon Cromwel's Return from Ireland

THE forward Youth that would appear
Must now forsake his *Muses* dear,
   Nor in the Shadows sing
   His Numbers languishing.
'Tis time to leave the Books in dust,   5
And oyl th' unused Armours rust,
   Removing from the Wall
   The Corslet of the Hall.
So restless *Cromwel* could not cease
In the inglorious Arts of Peace,   10
   But through adventrous War
   Urged his active Star.
And, like the three fork'd Lightning, first
Breaking the Clouds where it was nurst,
   Did thorough his own Side   15
   His fiery way divide.
For 'tis all one to Courage high
The Emulous or Enemy;
   And with such to inclose
   Is more then to oppose.   20

Then burning through the Air he went,
And Pallaces and Temples rent:
    And *Cæsars* head at last
    Did through his Laurels blast.
'Tis Madness to resist or blame   25
The force of angry Heavens flame:
    And, if we would speak true,
    Much to the Man is due.
Who, from his private Gardens, where
He liv'd reserved and austere,   30
    As if his highest plot
    To plant the Bergamot,
Could by industrious Valour climbe
To ruine the great Work of Time,
    And cast the Kingdome old   35
    Into another Mold.
Though Justice against Fate complain,
And plead the antient Rights in vain:
    But those do hold or break
    As Men are strong or weak.   40
Nature that hateth emptiness,
Allows of penetration less:
    And therefore must make room
    Where greater Spirits come.
What Field of all the Civil Wars,   45
Where his were not the deepest Scars?
    And *Hampton* shows what part
    He had of wiser Art.
Where, twining subtile fears with hope,
He wove a Net of such a scope,   50
    That *Charles* himself might chase
    To *Caresbrooks* narrow case.
That thence the *Royal Actor* born
The *Tragick Scaffold* might adorn:
    While round the armed Bands   55
    Did clap their bloody hands.

He nothing common did or mean
Upon that memorable Scene:
    But with his keener Eye
    The Axes edge did try: 60
Nor call'd the *Gods* with vulgar spight
To vindicate his helpless Right,
    But bow'd his comely Head,
    Down as upon a Bed.
This was that memorable Hour   65
Which first assur'd the forced Pow'r.
    So when they did design
    The *Capitols* first Line,
A bleeding Head where they begun,
Did fright the Architects to run;   70
    And yet in that the *State*
    Foresaw it's happy Fate.
And now the *Irish* are asham'd
To see themselves in one Year tam'd·
    So much one Man can do,   75
    That does both act and know.
They can affirm his Praises best,
And have, though overcome, confest
    How good he is, how just,
    And fit for highest Trust: 80
Nor yet grown stiffer with Command,
But still in the *Republick's* hand:
    How fit he is to sway
    That can so well obey.
He to the *Commons Feet* presents   85
A *Kingdome*, for his first years rents:
    And, what he may, forbears
    His Fame to make it theirs:
And has his Sword and Spoyls ungirt,
To lay them at the *Publick's* skirt.   90
    So when the Falcon high
    Falls heavy from the Sky,

She, having kill'd, no more does search,
But on the next green Bow to pearch;
    Where, when he first does lure,   **95**
    The Falckner has her sure.
What may not then our *Isle* presume
While Victory his Crest does plume!
    What may not others fear
    If thus he crown each Year!   **100**
A *Cæsar* he ere long to *Gaul*,
To *Italy* an *Hannibal*,
    And to all States not free
    Shall *Clymacterick* be.
The *Pict* no shelter now shall find   **105**
Within his party-colour'd Mind;
    But from this Valour sad
    Shrink underneath the Plad:
Happy if in the tufted brake
The *English Hunter* him mistake;   **110**
    Nor lay his Hounds in near
    The *Caledonian* Deer.
But thou the Wars and Fortunes Son
March indefatigably on:
    And for the last effect   **115**
    Still keep thy Sword erect;
Besides the force it has to fright
The Spirits of the shady Night,
    The same *Arts* that did *gain*
    A *Pow'r* must it *maintain*.   **120**

The First Anniversary
of the Government under *O.C.*

LIKE the vain Curlings of the Watry maze,
Which in smooth streams a sinking Weight does raise,

So Man, declining always, disappears
in the weak Circles of increasing Years;
And his short Tumults of themselves Compose, 5
While flowing Time above his Head does close.
 Cromwell alone with greater Vigour runs,
(Sun-like) the Stages of succeeding Suns:
And still the Day which he doth next restore,
Is the just Wonder of the Day before. 10
Cromwell alone doth with new Lustre spring,
And shines the Jewel of the yearly Ring.
 'Tis he the force of scattered Time contracts,
And in one Year the work of Ages acts:
While heavy Monarchs make a wide Return, 15
Longer, and more Malignant then *Saturn*:
And though they all *Platonique* years should raign
In the same Posture would be found again.
Their earthy Projects under ground they lay,
More slow and brittle then the *China* clay: 20
Well may they strive to leave them to their Son,
For one Thing never was by one King don.
Yet some more active for a Frontier Town
Took in by Proxie, beggs a false Renown;
Another triumphs at the publick Cost, 25
And will have Wonn, if he no more have Lost;
They fight by Others, but in Person wrong,
And only are against their Subjects strong;
Their other Wars seem but a feign'd contest,
This Common Enemy is still opprest; 30
If Conquerors, on them they turn their might;
If Conquered, on them they wreak their Spight:
They neither build the Temple in their dayes,
Nor Matter for succeeding Founders raise;
Nor sacred Prophecies consult within, 35
Much less themselves to perfect them begin;
No other care they bear of things above,
But with Astrologers, divine, and *Jove*,

122

To know how long their Planet yet Reprives
From the deserved Fate their guilty lives: 40
Thus (Image-like) an useless time they tell,
And with vain Scepter strike the hourly Bell;
Nor more contribute to the state of Things,
Then wooden Heads unto the Viols strings.

While indefatigable *Cromwell* hyes,   45
And cuts his way still nearer to the Skyes,
Learning a Musique in the Region clear,
To tune this lower to that higher Sphere.

So when *Amphion* did the Lute command,
Which the God gave him; with his gentle hand,   50
The rougher Stones, unto his Measures hew'd,
Dans'd up in order from the Quarreys rude;
This took a Lower, that an Higher place,
As he the Treble alter'd, or the Base:
No Note he struck, but a new Story lay'd,   55
And the great Work ascended while he play'd.

The listning Structures he with Wonder ey'd,
And still new Stopps to various Time apply'd:
Now through the Strings a Martial rage he throws,
And joining streight the *Theban* Tow'r arose;   60
Then as he strokes them with a Touch more sweet,
The flocking Marbles in a Palace meet;
But, for he most the graver Notes did try,
Therefore the Temples rear'd their Columns high:
Thus, ere he ceas'd, his sacred Lute creates   65
Th' harmonious City of the seven Gates.

Such was that wondrous Order and Consent,
When *Cromwell* tun'd the ruling Instrument;
While tedious Statesmen many years did hack,
Framing a Liberty that still went back;   70
Whose num'rous Gorge could swallow in an hour
That Island, which the Sea cannot devour:
Then our *Amphion* issues out and sings,
And once he struck, and twice, the pow'rful Strings.

The Commonwealth then first together came, 75
And each one enter'd in the willing Frame;
All other Matter yields, and may be rul'd;
But who the Minds of stubborn Men can build?
No Quarry bears a Stone so hardly wrought,
Nor with such labour from its Center brought; 80
None to be sunk in the Foundation bends,
Each in the House the highest Place contends,
And each the Hand that lays him will direct,
And some fall back upon the Architect;
Yet all compos'd by his attractive Song, 85
Into the Animated City throng.

The Common-wealth does through their Centers all
Draw the Circumf'rence of the publique Wall;
The crossest Spirits here do take their part,
Fast'ning the Contignation which they thwart; 90
And they, whose Nature leads them to divide,
Uphold, this one, and that the other Side;
But the most Equal still sustein the Height,
And they as Pillars keep the Work upright;
While the resistance of opposed Minds, 95
The Fabrick as with Arches stronger binds,
Which on the Basis of a Senate free,
Knit by the Roofs Protecting weight agree.

When for his Foot he thus a place had found,
He hurles e'er since the World about him round; 100
And in his sev'ral Aspects, like a Star,
Here shines in Peace, and thither shoots a War.
While by his Beams observing Princes steer,
And wisely court the Influence they fear;
O would they rather by his Pattern won. 105
Kiss the approaching, nor yet angry Son;
And in their numbred Footsteps humbly tread
The path where holy Oracles do lead;
How might they under such a Captain raise,
The great Designes kept for the latter Dayes! 110

But mad with Reason, so miscall'd, of State
They know them not, and what they know not, hate,
Hence still they sing Hosanna to the Whore,
And her whom they should Massacre adore:
But Indians whom they should convert, subdue;   115
Nor teach, but traffique with, or burn the Jew.

   Unhappy Princes, ignorantly bred,
By Malice some, by Errour more misled;
If gracious Heaven to my Life give length,
Leisure to Time, and to my Weakness Strength,   120
Then shall I once with graver Accents shake
Your Regal sloth, and your long Slumbers wake;
Like the shrill Huntsman that prevents the East,
Winding his Horn to Kings that chase the Beast.

   Till then my Muse shall hollow far behind   125
Angelique *Cromwell* who outwings the wind;
And in dark Nights and in cold Dayes alone
Pursues the Monster thorough every Throne:
Which shrinking to her *Roman* Den impure,
Gnashes her Goary teeth; nor there secure.   130

   Hence oft I think, if in some happy Hour
High Grace should meet in one with highest Pow'r,
And then a seasonable People still
Should bend to his, as he to Heavens will,
What we might hope, what wonderful Effect   135
From such a wish'd Conjuncture might reflect.
Sure, the mysterious Work, where none withstand,
Would forthwith finish under such a Hand:
Fore-shortned Time its useless Course would stay,
And soon precipitate the latest Day.   140
But a thick Cloud about that Morning lyes,
And intercepts the Beams of Mortal eyes,
That 'tis the most which we determine can,
If these the Times, then this must be the Man.
And well he therefore does, and well has guest,   145
Who in his Age has always forward prest:

And knowing not where Heaven's choice may light,
Girds yet his Sword, and ready stands to fight;
But Men alas, as if they nothing car'd,
Look on, all unconcern'd, or unprepar'd;   150
And Stars still fall, and still the Dragons Tail
Swinges the Volumes of its horrid Flail.
For the great Justice that did first suspend
The World by Sin, does by the same extend.
Hence that blest Day still counterpoysed wastes,   155
The Ill delaying, what th' Elected hastes;
Hence landing Nature to new Seas is tost,
And good Designes still with their Authors lost.

    And thou, great *Cromwell*, for whose happy birth
A Mold was chosen out of better Earth;   160
Whose Saint-like Mother we did lately see
Live out an Age, long as a Pedigree;
That she might seem, could we the Fall dispute,
T' have smelt the Blossome, and not eat the Fruit;
Though none does of more lasting Parents grow,   165
But never any did them Honor so;
Though thou thine Heart from Evil still unstain'd,
And always hast thy Tongue from fraud refrain'd;
Thou, who so oft through Storms of thundring Lead
Hast born securely thine undaunted Head,   170
Thy Brest through ponyarding Conspiracies,
Drawn from the Sheath of lying Prophecies;
Thee proof beyond all other Force or Skill,
Our Sins endanger, and shall one day kill.

    How near they fail'd, and in thy sudden Fall   175
At once assay'd to overturn us all.
Our brutish fury strugling to be Free,
Hurry'd thy Horses while they hurry'd thee.
When thou hadst almost quit thy Mortal cares,
And soyl'd in Dust thy Crown of silver Hairs.   180
Let this one Sorrow interweave among
The other Glories of our yearly Song.

Like skilful Looms which through the costly **thred**
Of purling Ore, a shining wave do shed:
So shall the Tears we on past Grief employ,   185
Still as they trickle, glitter in our Joy.
So with more Modesty we may be True,
And speak as of the Dead the Praises due:
While impious Men deceiv'd with pleasure short,
On their own Hopes shall find the Fall retort.   190
But the poor Beasts wanting their noble Guide,
What could they more? shrunk guiltily aside.
First winged Fear transports them far away,
And leaden Sorrow then their flight did stay.
See how they each his tow'ring Crest abate,   195
And the green Grass, and their known Mangers hate,
Nor through wide Nostrils snuffe the wanton air,
Nor their round Hoofs, or curled Mane's compare;
With wandring Eyes, and restless Ears they stood,
And with shrill Neighings ask'd him of the Wood.
Thou *Cromwell* falling, not a stupid Tree,   201
Or Rock so savage, but it mourn'd for thee:
And all about was heard a Panique groan,
As if that Nature's self were overthrown.
It seemed the Earth did from the Center tear;   205
It seemed the Sun was faln out of the Sphere:
Justice obstructed lay, and Reason fool'd;
Courage disheartened, and Religion cool'd.
A dismal Silence through the Palace went,
And then loud Shreeks the vaulted Marbles rent.   210
Such as the dying Chorus sings by turns,
And to deaf Seas, and ruthless Tempests mourns,
When now they sink, and now the plundring Streams
Break up each Deck, and rip the Oaken seams.
   But thee triumphant hence the firy Carr,   215
And firy Steeds had born out of the Warr,
From the low World, and thankless Men above,
Unto the Kingdom blest of Peace and Love:

We only mourn'd our selves, in thine Ascent,
Whom thou hadst left beneath with Mantle rent. 220
    For all delight of Life thou then didst lose,
When to Command, thou didst thy self Depose;
Resigning up thy Privacy so dear,
To turn the headstrong Peoples Charioteer;
For to be *Cromwell* was a greater thing, 225
Then ought below, or yet above a King:
Therefore thou rather didst thy Self depress,
Yielding to Rule, because it made thee Less.
    For, neither didst thou from the first apply
Thy sober Spirit unto things too High, 230
But in thine own Fields exercisedst long,
An healthful Mind within a Body strong;
Till at the Seventh time thou in the Skyes,
As a small Cloud, like a Mans hand didst rise;
Then did thick Mists and Winds the air deform, 235
And down at last thou pow'rdst the fertile Storm;
Which to the thirsty Land did plenty bring,
But though forewarn'd, o'r-took and wet the King.
    What since he did, an higher Force him push'd
Still from behind, and it before him rush'd, 240
Though undiscern'd among the tumult blind,
Who think those high Decrees by Man design'd.
'Twas Heav'n would not that his Pow'r should cease,
But walk still middle betwixt War and Peace;
Choosing each Stone, and poysing every weight, 245
Trying the Measures of the Bredth and Height;
Here pulling down, and there erecting New,
Founding a firm State by Proportions true.
    When *Gideon* so did from the War retreat,
Yet by the Conquest of two Kings grown great, 250
He on the Peace extends a Warlike power,
And *Is'rel* silent saw him rase the Tow'r;
And how he *Succouths* Elders durst suppress,
With Thorns and Briars of the Wilderness.

No King might ever such a Force have done;   255
Yet would not he be Lord, nor yet his Son.
    Thou with the same strength, and an Heart as plain,
Didst (like thine Olive) still refuse to Reign;
Though why should others all thy Labor spoil,
And Brambles be anointed with thine Oyl,   260
Whose climbing Flame, without a timely stop,
Had quickly Levell'd every Cedar's top.
Therefore first growing to thy self a Law,
Th' ambitious Shrubs thou in just time didst aw.
    So have I seen at Sea, when whirling Winds,   265
Hurry the Bark, but more the Seamens minds,
Who with mistaken Course salute the Sand,
And threat'ning Rocks misapprehend for Land;
While baleful *Tritons* to the shipwrack guide,
And Corposants along the Tacklings slide.   270
The Passengers all wearyed out before,
Giddy, and wishing for the fatal Shore;
Some lusty Mate, who with more careful Eye
Counted the Hours, and ev'ry Star did spy,
The Helm does from the artless Steersman strain,   275
And doubles back unto the safer Main.
What though a while they grumble discontent,
Saving himself he does their loss prevent.
    'Tis not a Freedome, that where All command;
Nor Tyranny, where One does them withstand: 280
But who of both the Bounders knows to lay
Him as their Father must the State obey.
    Thou, and thine House, like *Noah's* Eight did rest,
Left by the Wars Flood on the Mountains Crest:
And the large Vale lay subject to thy Will,   285
Which thou but as an Husbandman woulsd Till:
And only didst for others plant the Vine
Of Liberty, not drunken with its Wine.
    That sober Liberty which men may have,
That they enjoy, but more they vainly crave: **290**

And such as to their Parents Tents do press,
May shew their own, not see his Nakedness.
    Yet such a *Chammish* issue still does rage,
The Shame and Plague both of the Land and Age,
Who watch'd thy halting, and thy Fall deride,   295
Rejoycing when the Foot had slipt aside;
That their new King might the fifth Scepter shake,
And make the World, by his Example, Quake:
Whose frantique Army should they want for Men
Might muster Heresies, so one were ten.   300
What thy Misfortune, they the Spirit call,
And their Religion only is to Fall.
Oh! *Mahomet!* now couldst thou rise again,
Thy Falling-sickness should have made thee Reign,
While *Feake* and *Simpson* would in many a Tome,
Have writ the Comments of thy sacred Foame: 306
For soon thou mightst have past among their Rant
Wer't but for thine unmoved Tulipant;
As thou must needs have own'd them of thy band
For prophecies fit to be *Alcorand*.   310
    Accursed Locusts, whom your King does spit
Out of the Center of th' unbottom'd Pit;
Wand'rers, Adult'rers, Lyers, *Munser's* rest,
Sorcerers, Atheists, Jesuites, Possest;
You who the Scriptures and the Laws deface   315
With the same liberty as Points and Lace;
Oh Race most hypocritically strict!
Bent to reduce us to the ancient Pict;
Well may you act the *Adam* and the *Eve*;
Ay, and the Serpent too that did deceive.   320
    But the great Captain, now the danger's ore,
Makes you for his sake Tremble one fit more;
And, to your spight, returning yet alive
Does with himself all that is good revive.
    So when first Man did through the Morning new
See the bright Sun his shining Race pursue,   326

All day he follow'd with unwearied sight,
Pleas'd with that other World of moving Light;
But thought him when he miss'd his setting beams,
Sunk in the Hills, or plung'd below the Streams.   330
While dismal blacks hung round the Universe,
And Stars (like Tapers) burn'd upon his Herse:
And Owls and Ravens with their screeching noyse
Did make the Fun'rals sadder by their Joyes.
His weeping Eyes the doleful Vigils keep,   335
Not knowing yet the Night was made for sleep:
Still to the West, where he him lost, he turn'd,
And with such accents, as Despairing, mourn'd:
Why did mine Eyes once see so bright a Ray;
Or why Day last no longer then a Day?   340
When streight the Sun behind him he descry'd,
Smiling serenely from the further side.

So while our Star that gives us Light and Heat,
Seem'd now a long and gloomy Night to threat,
Up from the other World his Flame he darts,   345
And Princes shining through their windows starts;
Who their suspected Counsellors refuse,
And credulous Ambassadors accuse.

'Is this, saith one, the Nation that we read
'Spent with both Wars, under a Captain dead?   350
'Yet rig a Navy while we dress us late;
'And ere we Dine, rase and rebuild their State.
'What Oaken Forrests, and what golden Mines!
'What Mints of Men, what Union of Designes!
'Unless their Ships, do, as their Fowle proceed   355
'Of shedding Leaves, that with their Ocean breed.
'Theirs are not Ships, but rather Arks of War,
'And beaked Promontories sail'd from far;
'Of floting Islands a new Hatched Nest;
'A Fleet of Worlds, of other Worlds in quest;   360
'An hideous shole of wood-Leviathans,
'Arm'd with three Tire of brazen Hurricans;

'That through the Center shoot their thundring side
'And sink the Earth that does at Anchor ride.
'What refuge to escape them can be found,   365
'Whost watry Leaguers all the world surround?
'Needs must we all their Tributaries be,
'Whose Navies hold the Sluces of the Sea.
'The Ocean is the Fountain of Command,
'But that once took, we Captives are on Land.   370
'And those that have the Waters for their share,
'Can quickly leave us neither Earth nor Air.
'Yet if through these our Fears could find a pass;
'Through double Oak, & lin'd with treble Brass;
'That one Man still, although but nam'd, alarms   375
'More then all Men, all Navies, and all Arms.
'Him, all the Day, Him, in late Nights I dread,
'And still his Sword seems hanging o'er my head.
'The Nation had been ours, but his one Soul
'Moves the great Bulk, and animates the whole.   380
'He Secrecy with Number hath inchas'd,
'Courage with Age, Maturity with Hast:
'The Valiants Terror, Riddle of the Wise;
'And still his Fauchion all our Knots unties.
'Where did he learn those Arts that cost us dear?   385
'Where below Earth, or where above the Sphere?
'He seems a King by long Succession born,
'And yet the same to be a King does scorn.
'Abroad a King he seems, and something more,
'At home a Subject on the equal Floor.   390
'O could I once him with our Title see,
'So should I hope yet he might Dye as wee.
'But let them write his Praise that love him best,
'It grieves me sore to have thus much confest.

   Pardon, great Prince, if thus their Fear or Spight
More then our Love and Duty do thee Right.   396
I yield, nor further will the Prize contend;
So that we both alike may miss our End:

132

While thou thy venerable Head dost raise
As far above their Malice as my Praise.   **400**
And as the *Angel* of our Commonweal,
Troubling the Waters, yearly mak'st them Heal.

In Legationem Domini Oliveri St. John ad Provincias Fœderatas

INGENIOSA Viris contingunt Nomina magnis,
    Ut dubites Casu vel Ratione data.
Nam *Sors*, cæca licet, tamen est præsaga *futuri*;
    Et sub *fatidico Nomine* vera premit.
Et Tu, cui soli voluit *Respublica* credi,   **5**
    Fœdera seu *Belgis* seu nova Bella feras;
Haud frustra cecidit tibi Compellatio fallax,
    Ast scriptum *ancipiti Nomine* Munus erat;
Scilicet hoc *Martis*, sed *Pacis* Nuntius illo:
    Clavibus his *Jani* ferrea Claustra regis.   **10**
Non opus Arcanos Chartis committere Sensus,
    Et varia licitos condere Fraude Dolos.
Tu quoque si taceas tamen est *Legatio Nomen*
    Et velut in *Scytale* publica verba refert.
Vultis *Oliverum, Batavi, Sanctumve Johannem*?   **15**
    Antiochus gyro non breviore stetit.

A Letter to Doctor Ingelo, then with my Lord Whitlock, Ambassador from the Protector to the Queen of Sweden

QUID facis *Arctoi* charissime transfuga cœli,
    Ingele, proh serò cognite, rapte citò?
Num satis Hybernum defendis pellibus Astrum,

Qui modo tam mollis nec bene firmus eras?
Quæ Gentes Hominum, quæ sit Natura Locorum, 5
  Sint Homines, potius dic ibi sintne Loca?
Num gravis horrisono *Polus* obruit omnia lapsu,
  Jungitur & præceps Mundus utraque nive?
An melius canis horrescit Campus Aristis,
  Annuus Agricolis & redit Orbe labor? 10
Incolit, ut fertur, sævam Gens mitior Oram,
  Pace vigil, Bello strenua, justa Foro.
Quin ibi sunt *Urbes*, atque alta *Palatia Regum*,
  Musarumque domus, & sua *Templa Deo*.
Nam regit Imperio populum *Christina* ferocem, 15
  Et dare jura potest *regia Virgo* viris.
Utque trahit rigidum *Magnes* Aquilone Metallum,
  Gaudet eam Soboles ferrea sponte sequi.
Dic quantum liceat fallaci credere Famæ,
  Invida num taceat plura, sonetve loquax. 20
At, si vera fides, Mundi melioris ab ortu,
  Sæcula *Christinæ* nulla tulere parem.
Ipsa licet redeat (nostri decus orbis) *Eliza*,
  Qualis nostra tamen quantaque *Eliza* fuit.
Vidimus Effigiem, mistasque Coloribus Umbras: 25
  Sic quoque *Sceptripotens*, sic quoque visa *Dea*.
Augustam decorant (raro concordia) frontem
  Majestas & Amor, Forma Pudorque simul.
Ingens Virgineo spirat *Gustavus* in ore:
  Agnoscas animos, fulmineumque Patrem. 30
Nulla suo nituit tam lucida Stella sub Axe;
  Non Ea quæ meruit Crimine *Nympha* Polum.
Ah quoties pavidum demisit conscia Lumen,
  Utque suæ timuit *Parrhasis* Ora *Deæ*!
Et, simulet falsa ni Pictor imagine Vultus, 35
  Delia tam similis nec fuit ipsa sibi.
Ni quod inornati *Triviæ* sint forte Capilli,
  Sollicita sed huic distribuantur Acu.
Scilicet ut nemo est illa reverentior æqui;
  Haud ipsas igitur fert sine Lege Comas. 40

134

Gloria sylvarum pariter communis utrique
    Est, & perpetuæ Virginitatis Honos.
Sic quoque *Nympharum* supereminet Agmina collo,
    Fertque *Choros Cynthi* per Juga, perque Nives.
Haud aliter pariles Ciliorum contrahit Arcus   45
    Acribus ast Oculis tela subesse putes.
Luminibus dubites an straverit illa Sagittis
    Quæ fovet exuviis ardua colla Feram.
Alcides humeros coopertus *pelle Nemæa*
    Haud ita labentis sustulit Orbis Onus.   50
Heu quæ Cervices subnectunt Pectora tales,
    Frigidiora Gelu, candidiora Nive.
Cætera non licuit, sed vix ea tota, videre;
    Nam clausi rigido stant *Adamante* Sinus.
Seu Chlamys Artifici nimium succurrerit auso,   55
    Sicque imperfectum fugerit impar Opus:
Sive tribus spernat Victrix certare *Deabus,*
    Et pretium formæ nec spoliata ferat.
Junonis properans & clara Trophæa *Minervæ;*
    Mollia nam *Veneris* præmia nosse piget.   60
Hinc neque consuluit fugitivæ prodiga Formæ,
    Nec timuit seris invigilasse Libris.
Insomnem quoties *Nymphæ* monuere sequaces
    Decedet roseis heu color ille Genis.
Jamque vigil leni cessit *Philomela* sopori,   65
    Omnibus & Sylvis conticuere Feræ.
Acrior illa tamen pergit, Curasque fatigat:
    Tanti est doctorum volvere scripta Virum.
Et liciti quæ sint moderamina discere Regni,
    Quid fuerit, quid sit, noscere quicquid erit.   70
Sic quod in ingenuas *Gothus* peccaverit Artes
    Vindicat, & studiis expiat *Una* suis.
Exemplum dociles imitantur nobile Gentes,
    Et geminis Infans imbuit Ora sonis.
Transpositos *Suecis* credas migrasse *Latinos,*   75
    Carmine Romuleo sic strepit omne Nemus.
Upsala nec priscis impar memoratur *Athenis,*

Ægidaque & Curris hic sua *Pallas* habet.
Illinc O quales liceat sperasse Liquores,
    Quum *Dea* præsideat fontibus ipsa sacris!   80
Illic Lacte ruant illic & flumina Melle,
    Fulvaque inauratam tingat Arena *Salam.*
Upsalides Musæ nunc & majora canemus,
    Quæque mihi Famæ non levis Aura tulit.
Creditur haud ulli *Christus* signasse suorum   85
    Occultam gemma de meliore Notam.
Quemque tenet charo descriptum *Nomine* semper,
    Non minus exculptum Pectore fida refert.
Sola hæc virgineas depascit Flamma Medullas,
    Et licito pergit solvere corda foco.   90
Tu quoque Sanctorum fastos *Christina* sacrabis,
    Unica nec *Virgo Volsiniensis* erit.
Discite nunc *Reges* (*Majestas proxima cælo*)
    Discite proh magnos hinc coluisse *Deos.*
Ah pudeat Tantos puerilia fingere cœpta,   95
    Nugas nescio quas, & male quærere Opes.
Acer *Equo* cunctos dum præterit ille *Britanno,*
    Et pecoris spolium nescit inerme sequi.
Ast *Aquilam* poscit *Germano* pellere *Nido,*
    Deque *Palatino* Monte fugare *Lupam.*   100
Vos etiam latos in prædam jungite *Campos,*
    Impiaque arctatis cingite Lustra Plagis.
Victor Oliverus nudum Caput exerit Armis,
    Ducere sive sequi nobile lætus Iter.
Qualis jam *Senior* Solymæ *Godfredus* ad Arces,
    Spina cui canis floruit alba Comis.   106
Et *Lappos Christina* potest & solvere *Finnos,*
    Ultima quos *Boreæ* carcere Claustra premunt.
Æoliis quales Venti fremuere sub antris,
    Et tentant Montis corripuisse moras.   110
Hanc *Dea* si summa demiserit Arce procellam
    Quam gravis *Austriacis Hesperiisque* cadat!
Omnia sed rediens olim narraveris Ipse;
    Nec reditus spero tempora longa petit.

Non ibi lenta pigro stringuntur frigore Verba, 115
  Solibus, & tandem Vere liquanda novo.
Sed radiis hyemem *Regina* potentior urit;
  Hæcque magis solvit, quam ligat illa Polum.
Dicitur & nostros mœrens audisse Labores,
  Fortis & ingenuam Gentis amasse Fidem.   120
Oblatæ *Batavam* nec paci commodat *Aurem*;
  Nec versat *Danos* insidiosa *dolos*.
Sed pia festinat mutatis Fœdera rebus,
  Et *Libertatem* quæ dominatur amat.
Dĭgnă cŭī *Salomon* meritos retulisset honores, 125
  Et *Saba* concretum Thure cremasset Iter.
Hanc tua, sed melius, celebraverit, *Ingele, Musa*;
  Et labor est vestræ debitus ille Lyræ.
Nos sine te frustra *Thamisis* saliceta subimus,
  Sparsaque per steriles Turba vagamur Agros.
Et male tentanti querulum respondet Avena: 131
  Quin & *Rogerio* dissiluere fides.
Hæc tamen absenti memores dictamus *Amico*,
  Grataque speramus qualiacumque fore.

In Effigiem Oliveri Cromwell

HAEC est quæ toties *Inimicos* Umbra fugavit,
At sub qua *Cives* Otia lenta terunt.

In eandem Reginæ Sueciæ transmissam

BELLIPOTENS Virgo, septem Regina Trionum.
  Christina, Arctoi lucida stella Poli;
Cernis quas merui dura sub Casside Rugas;
  Sicque *Senex* Armis impiger Ora fero;

Invia Fatorum dum per Vestigia nitor,
 Exequor & Populi fortia Jussa Manu.
At tibi submittit frontem reverentior *Umbra*,
 Nec sunt *hi Vultus* Regibus usque truces.

Two Songs
at the Marriage of the Lord Fauconberg and the Lady Mary Cromwell

First

Chorus. Endymion. Luna

Chorus

Th' *Astrologers* own Eyes are set,
And even Wolves the Sheep forget;
Only *this Shepheard*, late and soon,
Upon this Hill outwakes the *Moon*.
Heark how he sings, with sad delight,   5
Thorough the clear and silent Night.

Endymion

Cynthia, O Cynthia, turn thine Ear,
Nor scorn *Endymions* plaints to hear.
As we our Flocks, so you command
The fleecy Clouds with silver wand.   10

Cynthia

If thou a *Mortal*, rather sleep;
Or if a *Shepheard*, watch thy Sheep.

Endymion

The *Shepheard*, since he saw thine Eyes,
And *Sheep* are both thy *Sacrifice*.
Nor merits he a *Mortal's* name,   **15**
That burns with an *immortal Flame.*

Cynthia

I have enough for me to do,
Ruling the Waves that Ebb and flow.

Endymion

Since thou disdain'st not then to share
On Sublunary things thy care;   **20**
Rather restrain these double Seas,
Mine Eyes uncessant deluges.

Cynthia

My wakeful Lamp all night must move,
Securing their Repose above.

Endymion

If therefore thy resplendent Ray   **25**
Can make a Night more bright then Day;
Shine thorough this obscurer Brest,
With shades of deep Despair opprest.

Chorus

Courage, *Endymion*, boldly Woo,
Anchises was a *Shepheard* too: **30**
Yet is *her younger Sister* laid
Sporting with him in *Ida's shade*:
   And *Cynthia*, though the strongest
Seeks but the honour to have held out longest.

Endymion

Here unto *Latmos Top* I climbe: 35
How far below thine *Orbe* sublime?
O why, as well as Eyes to see,
Have I not Armes that reach to thee?

Cynthia

'Tis needless then that I refuse,
Would you but your own Reason use.   40

Endymion

Though I so high may not pretend,
It is the same so you descend.

Cynthia

These Stars would say I do them wrong,
Rivals each one for thee too strong.

Endymion

The Stars are fix'd unto their *Sphere*,   45
And cannot, though they would, come near.
Less Loves set of each others praise,
While *Stars* Eclipse by mixing Rayes.

Cynthia

That Cave is dark.

Endymion

　　　Then none can spy: 50
Or shine Thou there and 'tis the Sky.

Chorus

Joy to *Endymion*,
For he has *Cynthia's* favour won.

And *Jove* himself approves
With his serenest influence their Loves.   55
  For he did never love to pair
  His Progeny above the Air;
  But to be honest, valiant, wise,
Makes *Mortals* matches fit for *Deityes.*

Second Song

Hobbinol. Phillis. Tomalin

Hobbinol

PHILLIS, Tomalin, away:
Never such a merry day.
For *the Northern Shepheards Son*
Has *Menalca's daughter* won.

Phillis

Stay till I some flow'rs ha' ty'd   **5**
In a Garland for the Bride.

Tomalin

If thou would'st a Garland bring,
Phillis you may wait the Spring:
They ha' chosen such an hour
When *She* is the only flow'r.   **10**

Phillis

Let's not then at least be seen
Without each a Sprig of Green.

Hobbinol

Fear not; at *Menalca's Hall.*
There is Bayes enough for all.

He when Young as we did graze,   15
But when Old he planted Bayes.

Tomalin

Here *She* comes; but with a Look
Far more catching then my Hook.
'Twas those Eyes, I now dare swear,
Led our Lambs we knew not where.   20

Hobbinol

Not our Lambs own Fleeces are
Curl'd so lovely as her Hair:
Nor our Sheep new Wash'd can be
Half so white or sweet as *She*.

Phillis

He so looks as fit to keep   25
Somewhat else then silly *Sheep*.

Hobbinol

Come, lets in some Carol new
Pay to Love and Them their due.

All

Joy to that *happy Pair*,
Whose Hopes united banish our Despair.   30
What *Shepheard* could for Love pretend,
Whil'st all the *Nymphs* on *Damon's* choice
    attend?
What *Shepherdess* could hope to wed
Before *Marina's* turn were sped?
Now lesser Beauties may take place,   35
And meaner Virtues come in play;

While they,
Looking from high,
Shall grace

Our Flocks and us with a propitious Eye.   **40**
    But what is most, the gentle Swain
    No more shall need of Love complain;
    But Virtue shall be Beauties hire,
And those be equal that have equal Fire.
    Marina yields. Who dares be coy?   **45**
Or who despair, now *Damon* does enjoy?
      Joy to that happy Pair,
Whose Hopes united banish our Despair.

A Poem upon the Death of O. C.

THAT Providence which had so long the care
Of *Cromwell's* head, and numbred ev'ry hair,
Now in its self (the Glass where all appears)
Had seen the period of his golden Years:
And thenceforth onely did attend to trace,   **5**
What death might least so fair a Life deface.
    The People, which what most they fear esteem,
Death when more horrid so more noble deem;
And blame the last *Act*, like *Spectators* vain,
Unless the *Prince* whom they applaud be slain.   **10**
Nor Fate indeed can well refuse that right
To those that liv'd in War, to dye in Fight.
    But long his *Valour* none had left that could
Indanger him, or *Clemency* that would.
And he whom Nature all for Peace had made,   **15**
But angry Heaven unto War had sway'd,
And so less useful where he most desir'd,
For what he least affected was admir'd,
Deserved yet an End whose ev'ry part
Should speak the wondrous softness of his Heart. **20**

To *Love* and *Grief* the fatal Writ was sign'd;
(Those nobler weaknesses of humane Mind,
From which those Powers that issu'd the Decree,
Although immortal, found they were not free.)
That they, to whom his Breast still open lyes,   25
In gentle Passions should his Death disguise:
And leave succeeding Ages cause to mourn,
As long as Grief shall weep, or Love shall burn.

   Streight does a slow and languishing Disease
Eliza, Natures and his darling, seize.   30
Her when an infant, taken with her Charms,
He oft would flourish in his mighty Arms;
And, lest their force the tender burthen wrong,
Slacken the vigour of his Muscles strong;
Then to the Mothers brest her softly move,   35
Which while she drain'd of Milk she filled with Love.
But as with riper Years her Virtue grew,
And ev'ry minute adds a Lustre new;
When with meridian height her Beauty shin'd,
And thorough that sparkled her fairer Mind;   40
When She with Smile serene and Words discreet
His hidden Soul at ev'ry turn could meet;
Then might y' ha' daily his Affection spy'd,
Doubling that knot which Destiny had ty'd.
While they by sence, not knowing, comprehend   45
How on each other both their Fates depend.
With her each day the pleasing Hours he shares,
And at her Aspect calms his growing Cares;
Or with a Grandsire's joy her Children sees
Hanging about her neck or at his knees.   50
Hold fast dear Infants, hold them both or none;
This will not stay when once the other's gone.

   A silent fire now wasts those Limbs of Wax,
And him within his tortur'd Image racks.
So the Flowr with'ring which the Garden crown'd,   55
The sad Root pines in secret under ground.

Each Groan he doubled and each Sigh he sigh'd,
Repeated over to the restless Night.
No trembling String compos'd to Numbers new,
Answers the touch in Notes more sad more true.   60
She lest He grieve hides what She can her pains,
And He to lessen hers his Sorrow feigns:
Yet both perceiv'd, yet both conceal'd their Skills,
And so diminishing increast their ills:
That whether by each others grief they fell,   65
Or on their own redoubled, none can tell.

   And now *Eliza's* purple Locks were shorn,
Where She so long her *Father's* fate had worn:
And frequent lightning to her Soul that flyes,
Devides the Air, and opens all the Skyes: 70
And now his Life, suspended by her breath,
Ran out impetuously to hasting Death.
Like polish'd Mirrours, so his steely Brest
Had ev'ry figure of her woes exprest;
And with the damp of her last Gasps obscur'd,   75
Had drawn such staines as were not to be cur'd.
Fate could not either reach with single stroke,
But the dear Image fled the Mirrour broke.

   Who now shall tell us more of mournful Swans,
Of Halcyons kind, or bleeding Pelicans?   80
No downy breast did ere so gently beat,
Or fan with airy plumes so soft an heat.
For he no duty by his height excus'd,
Nor though a *Prince* to be a *Man* refused:
But rather then in his *Eliza's* pain   85
Not love, not grieve, would neither live nor reign:
And in himself so oft immortal try'd,
Yet in compassion of another dy'd.

   So have I seen a Vine, whose lasting Age
Of many a Winter hath surviv'd the rage.   90
Under whose shady tent Men ev'ry year
At its rich bloods expence their Sorrows chear

If some dear branch where it extends its life
Chance to be prun'd by an untimely knife,
The Parent-Tree unto the Grief succeeds,   95
And through the Wound its vital humour bleeds;
Trickling in watry drops, whose flowing shape
Weeps that it falls ere fix'd into a Grape.
So the dry Stock, no more that spreading Vine,
Frustrates the Autumn and the hopes of Wine.   100
   A secret Cause does sure those Signs ordain
Fore boding Princes falls, and seldom vain.
Whether some Kinder Pow'rs, that wish us well,
What they above cannot prevent, foretell;
Or the great World do by consent presage,   105
As hollow Seas with future Tempests rage:
Or rather Heav'n, which us so long foresees,
Their fun'rals celebrates while it decrees.
But never yet was any humane Fate
By nature solemniz'd with so much state.   110
He unconcern'd the dreadful passage crost;
But oh what pangs that Death did Nature cost!
First the great *Thunder* was shot off, and sent
The Signal from the starry Battlement.
The *Winds* receive it, and its force out-do,   115
As practising how they could thunder too:
Out of the Binders Hand the Sheaves they tore,
And thrash'd the Harvest in the airy floore;
Or of huge Trees, whose growth with his did rise,
The deep foundations open'd to the Skyes.   120
Then heavy *Showres* the winged Tempests lead,
And pour the Deluge ore the *Chaos* head.
The Race of warlike *Horses* at his Tomb
Offer themselves in many a *Hecatomb*;
With pensive head towards the ground they fall,   125
And helpless languish at the tainted Stall.
Numbers of *Men* decrease with pains unknown
And hasten not to see his Death their own.

146

Such Tortures all the Elements unfix'd,
Troubled to part where so exactly mix'd. 130
And as through Air his wasting Spirits flow'd,
The Universe labour'd beneath their load.

　　Nature it seem'd with him would Nature vye;
He with *Eliza*, It with him would dye.

　　He without noise still travell'd to his End, 135
As silent Suns to meet the Night descend.
The *Stars* that for him fought had only pow'r
Left to determine now his fatal Hour;
Which, since they might not hinder, yet they cast
To chuse it worthy of his *Glories* past. 140

　　No part of time but bore his mark away
Of honour; all the Year was *Cromwell's* day:
But this, of all the most auspicious found,
Twice had in open field him Victor crown'd:
When up the armed Mountains of *Dunbar* 145
He march'd, and through deep *Severn* ending war.
What day should him *eternize* but the same
That had before *immortaliz'd* his *Name*?
That so who ere would at his Death have joy'd,
In their own Griefs might find themselves imploy'd;
But those that sadly his departure griev'd, 151
Yet joy'd remembring what he once atchiev'd.
And the last minute his victorious *Ghost*
Gave chase to *Ligney* on the *Belgick Coast*.
Here ended all his mortal toyles: He lay'd 155
And slept in Peace under the *Lawrel shade*.

　　O Cromwell, Heavens Favorite! To none
Have such high honours from above been shown:
For whom the Elements we Mourners see,
And *Heav'n* it self would the great *Herald* be; 160
Which with more Care set forth his Obsequies
Then those of *Moses* hid from humane Eyes;
As jealous only here lest all be less,
That we could to his Memory express.

Then let us to our course of Mourning keep: 165
Where *Heaven* leads, 'tis Piety to weep.
Stand back ye Seas, and shrunk beneath the vail
Of your *Abysse*, with cover'd Head bewail
Your *Monarch*: We demand not your supplies
To compass in our *Isle*; our Tears suffice: 170
Since him away the dismal Tempest rent,
Who once more joyn'd us to the Continent;
Who planted *England* on the *Flandrick shoar*,
And stretched *our frontire* to the *Indian Ore*;
Whose greater *Truths* obscure the *Fables* old,   175
Whether of *Brittish Saints or Worthy's* told;
And in a valour less'ning *Arthur's* deeds,
For Holyness the *Confessor* exceeds.

    He first put Armes into *Religions* hand,
And tim'rous *Conscience* unto *Courage* man'd: 180
The Souldier taught that inward Mail to wear,
And *fearing God* how they should *nothing fear*.
Those Strokes he said will pierce through all below
Where those that strike from Heaven fetch their Blow.
Astonish'd armyes did their flight prepare,   185
And Cityes strong were stormed by his prayer;
Of that for ever *Preston's* field shall tell
The story, and impregnable *Clonmell*.
And where the sandy mountain *Fenwick* scal'd,
The sea between, yet hence his pray'r prevail'd.   190
What man was ever so in Heav'n obey'd
Since the commanded sun o're *Gibeon* stay'd?
In all his warrs needs must he triumph, when
He conquer'd *God*, still ere he fought with men:
Hence, though in battle none so brave or fierce,   195
Yet him the adverse steel could never pierce.
Pity it seem'd to hurt him more that felt
Each wound himself which he to others delt;
Danger itself refusing to offend
So loose an enemy, so fast a friend.   200

Friendship, that sacred virtue, long dos claime
The first foundation of his house and name:
But within one its narrow limits fall,
His tendernesse extended unto all.
And that deep soule through every channell flows, 205
Where kindly nature loves itself to lose.
More strong affections never reason serv'd,
Yet still affected most what best deserv'd.
If he *Eliza* lov'd to that degree,
(Though who more worthy to be lov'd than she?) 210
If so indulgent to his own, how deare
To him the children of the Highest were?
For her he once did nature's tribute pay:
For these his life adventur'd every day:
And 'twould be found, could we his thoughts have
    cast, 215
Their griefs struck deepest, if *Eliza's* last.
  What prudence more than humane did he need
To keep so deare, so diff'ring mindes agreed?
The worser sort, so conscious of their ill,
Lye weak and easy to the ruler's will; 220
But to the good (too many or too few)
All law is uselesse, all reward is due.
Oh ill advis'd, if not for love, for shame,
Spare yet your own, if you neglect his fame;
Least others dare to think your zeale a maske, 225
And you to govern only Heaven's taske.
  Valour, religion, friendship, prudence dy'd
At once with him, and all that's good beside;
And we death's refuse Nature's dregs confin'd
To loathsome life, Alas! are left behind 230
Where we (so once we us'd) shall now no more,
To fetch day, presse about his chamber-door;
From which he issu'd with that awfull state,
It seem'd Mars broke through *Janus'* double gate;
Yet always temper'd with an Aire so mild, 235
No *April* sunns that ere so gently smil'd;

No more shall heare that powerful language charm,
Whose force oft spar'd the labour of his arm:
No more shall follow where he spent the dayes
In warre, in counsell, or in pray'r, and praise;   240
Whose meanest acts he would himself advance,
As ungirt *David* to the arke did dance.
All, all is gone of ours or his delight
In horses fierce, wild deer, or armour bright;
Francisca faire can nothing now but weep,   245
Nor with soft notes shall sing his cares asleep.

I saw him dead, a leaden slumber lyes,
And mortal sleep over those wakefull eyes:
Those gentle Rays under the lids were fled,
Which through his looks that piercing sweetnesse
        shed;   250
That port which so Majestique was and strong,
Loose and depriv'd of vigour, stretch'd along:
All wither'd, all discolour'd, pale and wan,
How much another thing, no more that man?
Oh humaine glory, vaine, Oh death, oh wings,   255
Oh worthlesse world oh transitory things!
Yet dwelt that greatnesse in his shape decay'd
That still though dead, greater than death he lay'd;
And in his alter'd face you something faigne,
That threatens death, he yet will live againe.   260

Not much unlike the sacred Oak, which shoots
To Heav'n its branches, and through earth its roots:
Whose spacious boughs are hung with Trophies round,
And honour'd wreaths have oft the victour crown'd.
When angry *Jove* darts lightning through the Aire,
At mortalls sins, nor his own plant will spare;   266
(It groans, and bruises all below that stood
So many yeares the shelter of the wood.)
The tree ere while foreshortned to our view,
When fall'n shews taller yet than as it grew: 270

So shall his praise to after times increase,
When truth shall be allow'd, and faction cease;

And his own shadows with him fall; the eye
Detracts from objects than itself more high:
But when death takes them from that envy'd Seate,
Seeing how little we confess, how greate;   276
Thee, many ages hence, in martial verse
Shall th' *English* souldier, ere he charge, rehearse;
Singing of thee, inflame themselves to fight,
And with the name of *Cromwell*, armyes fright.   280
As long as rivers to the seas shall runne,
As long as *Cynthia* shall relieve the sunne,
While staggs shall fly unto the forests thick,
While sheep delight the grassy downs to pick,
As long as future time succeeds the past,   285
Always thy honour, praise and name, shall last.

   Thou in a pitch how farre beyond the sphere
Of humane glory towr'st, and raigning there
Despoyl'd of mortall robes, in seas of blisse,
Plunging dost bathe and tread the bright abysse: 290
There thy great soule at once a world does see,
Spacious enough, and pure enough for thee.
How soon thou *Moses* hast, and *Joshua* found,
And *David*, for the sword and harpe renown'd?
How streight canst to each happy mansion goe?   295
(Farr better known above than here below:)
And in those joyes dost spend the endlesse day,
Which in expressing, we ourselves betray.

   For we, since thou art gone, with heavy doome,
Wander like ghosts about thy loved tombe;   300
And lost in tears, have neither sight nor minde
To guide us upward through this Region blinde.
Since thou art gone, who best that way could'st teach,
Onely our sighs, perhaps, may thither reach.

   And *Richard* yet, where his great Parent led,   305
Beats on the rugged track: He, vertue dead,
Revives; and by his milder beams assures;
And yet how much of them his griefe obscures.

He, as his father, long was kept from sight
In private, to be view'd by better light;   310
But open'd once, what splendour dos he throw?
A *Cromwell* in an houre a prince will grow.
How he becomes that seat, how strongly streins,
How gently winds at once the ruling Reins?
Heav'n to this choice prepar'd a Diadem,   315
Richer then any Eastern silk, or gemme;
A pearly rainbow, where the Sun inchas'd
His brows, like an Imperiall Jewel grac'd.

We find already what those Omens mean,
Earth nere more glad, nor Heaven more serene.   320
Cease now our griefs, calme peace succeeds a war,
Rainbow to storms, *Richard* to *Oliver*.
Tempt not his clemency to try his pow'r,
He threats no Deluge, yet foretells a showre.

ADDITIONAL POEMS

To his Noble Friend Mr. Richard Lovelace, upon his Poems

Sir,

Our times are much degenerate from those
Which your sweet Muse which your fair Fortune
   chose,
And as complexions alter with the Climes,
Our wits have drawne th' infection of our times.
That candid Age no other way could tell   5
To be ingenious, but by speaking well.
Who best could prayse, had then the greatest prayse,
Twas more esteemed to give, then weare the Bayes:
Modest ambition studi'd only then,
To honour not her selfe, but worthy men.   10
These vertues now are banisht out of Towne,
Our Civill Wars have lost the Civicke crowne.
He highest builds, who with most Art destroys,
And against others Fame his owne employs,
I see the envious Caterpillar sit   15
On the faire blossome of each growing wit.
   The Ayre's already tainted with the swarms
Of Insects which against you rise in arms.
Word-peckers, Paper-rats, Book-scorpions,
Of wit corrupted, the unfashion'd Sons.   20
The barbed Censurers begin to looke
Like the grim consistory on thy Booke;
And on each line cast a reforming eye,
Severer then the young Presbytery.
Till when in vaine they have thee all perus'd,   25
You shall for being faultlesse be accus'd.
Some reading your *Lucasta*, will alledge
You wrong'd in her the Houses Priviledge.
Some that you under sequestration are,
Because you write when going to the Warre,   30

155

And one the Book prohibits, because *Kent*
Their first Petition by the Authour sent.
   But when the beauteous Ladies came to know
That their deare *Lovelace* was endanger'd so:
Lovelace that thaw'd the most congealed brest,   35
He who lov'd best and them defended best.
Whose hand so rudely grasps the steely brand,
Whose hand so gently melts the Ladies hand.
They all in mutiny though yet undrest
Sally'd and would in his defence contest.   40
And one the loveliest that was yet e're seen,
Thinking that I too of the rout had been,
Mine eyes invaded with a female spight
(She knew what pain 'twould be to lose that sight.)
O no, mistake not, I reply'd, for I   45
In your defence, or in his cause would dy.
But he secure of glory and of time
Above their envy, or mine aid doth clime.
Him, valiant men, and fairest Nymphys approve,
His Booke in them finds Judgement, with you
      Love.   50

                      ANDR. MARVELL

Upon the Death of the Lord Hastings

Go, intercept some Fountain in the Vein,
Whose Virgin-Source yet never steept the Plain
Hastings is dead, and we must finde a Store
Of Tears untoucht, and never wept before.
Go, stand betwixt the *Morning* and the *Flowers*;   5
And, ere they fall, arrest the early *Showers.*
Hastings is dead; and we, disconsolate,
With early *Tears* must morn his early *Fate.*

Alas, his *Vertues* did his *Death* presage:
Needs must he die, that doth out-run his *Age*.　10
The Phlegmatick and Slowe prolongs his day,
And on Times Wheel sticks like a *Remora*.
What man is he, that hath not *Heaven* beguil'd,
And is not thence mistaken for a *Childe*?
While those of growth more sudden, and more bold,
Are hurried hence, as if already old.　16
For, there above, They number not as here,
But weigh to Man the *Geometrick* yeer.

Had he but at this Measure still increast,
And on *the Tree of Life* once made a Feast,　20
As that of *Knowledge*; what Loves had he given
To Earth, and then what Jealousies to Heaven!
But 't is a *Maxime* of that State, That none,
Lest He become like Them, taste more than one.
Therefore the *Democratick* Stars did rise,　25
And all that Worth from hence did *Ostracize*.

Yet as some *Prince*, that, for State-Jealousie,
Secures his neerest and most lov'd *Ally*;
His Thought with richest Triumphs entertains,
And in the choicest Pleasures charms his Pains:　30
So he, not banisht hence, but there confin'd,
There better recreates his active Minde.

Before the *Chrystal Palace* where he dwells
The armed *Angels* hold their Carouzels;
And underneath, he views the *Turnaments*　35
Of all these Sublunary *Elements*.
But most he doth th' *Eternal Book* behold,
On which the *happie Names* do stand enroll'd;
And gladly there can all his Kindred claim,
But most rejoyces at his *Mothers* name.　40

The gods themselves cannot their Joy conceal,
But draw their Veils, and their pure Beams reveal:
Onely they drooping *Hymeneus* note,
Who for sad *Purple* tears his *Saffron*-coat;

And trails his Torches th'row the Starry Hall   45
Reversed, at his *Darlings* Funeral.
   And *Æsculapius*, who, asham'd and stern,
Himself at once condemneth, and *Mayern*;
Like some sad *Chymist*, who, prepar'd to reap
The *Golden Harvest*, sees his Glasses leap.   50
For, how Immortal must their race have stood,
Had *Mayern* once been mixt with *Hastings* blood!
How Sweet and Verdant would these *Lawrels* be,
Had they been planted on that *Balsam*-tree!
   But what could he, good man, although he bruis'd
All Herbs, and them a thousand ways infus'd?   56
All he had try'd, but all in vain, he saw,
And wept, as we, without Redress or Law.
For *Man* (alas) is but the *Heavens* sport;
And *Art* indeed is Long, but *Life* is Short.   60

ANDREW MARVEL

An Elegy upon the Death of my Lord Francis Villiers

Tis true that he is dead: but yet to chuse,
Methinkes thou Fame should not have brought the
   news
Thou canst discourse at will and speak at large:
But wast not in the fight nor durst thou charge.
While he transported all with valient rage   5
His Name eternizd, but cut short his age;
On the safe battlements of Richmonds bowers
Thou was espyd, and from the guilded Towers
Thy silver Trumpets sounded a Retreat,
Farre from the dust and battails sulphry heat.   10
Yet what couldst thou have done? 'tis always late
To struggle with inevitable fate.

Much rather thou I know expectst to tell
How heavy *Cromwell* gnasht the earth and fell.
Or how slow Death farre from the sight of day   15
The long-deceived *Fairfax* bore away.
But untill then, let us young *Francis* praise:
And plant upon his hearse the bloody bayes,
Which we will water with our welling eyes.
Teares spring not still from spungy Cowardice.   20
The purer fountains from the Rocks more steep
Destill and stony valour best doth weep.
Besides Revenge, if often quencht in teares,
Hardens like Steele and daily keener weares.

   Great *Buckingham* whose death doth freshy strike
Our memoryes, because to this so like;   26
Ere that in the Eternal Court he shone,
And here a Favorite there found a throne;
The fatall night before he hence did bleed,
Left to his *Princess* this immortal seed.   30
As the wise *Chinese* in the fertile wombe
Of Earth doth a more precious clay entombe,
Which dying by his will he leaves consigned:
Till by mature delay of time refind
The christall metall fit to the releast   35
Is taken forth to crowne each royal feast:
Such was the fate by which this Postume breathed
Who scarcely seems begotten but bequeathd.

   Never was any humane plant that grew
More faire then this and acceptably new.   40
'Tis truth that beauty doth most men dispraise:
Prudence and valour their esteeme do raise.
But he that hath already these in store,
Can not be poorer sure for having more.
And his unimitable handsomenesse   45
Made him indeed be more then man, not less.
We do but faintly gods resemblance beare
And like rough coyns of carelesse mints appeare:

But he of purpose made, did represent
In a rich Medall every lineament.   50
    Lovely and admirable as he was,
Yet was his Sword or Armour all his Glasse.
Nor in his Mistris eyes that joy he tooke,
As in an Enemies himselfe to looke.
I know how well he did, with what delight   55
Those serious imitations of fight.
Still in the trialls of strong exercise
His was the first, and his the second prize.
    Bright Lady, thou that rulest from above
The last and greatest Monarchy of Love: 60
Faire *Richmond* hold thy Brother or he goes.
Try if the Jasmin of thy hand or Rose
Of thy red Lip can keep him always here.
For he loves danger and doth never feare.
Or may thy tears prevaile with him to stay?   65
    But he resolv'd breaks carelessly away.
Onely one argument could now prolong
His stay and that most faire and so most strong:
The matchlesse *Chlora* whose pure fires did warm
His soule and only could his passions charme.   70
    You might with much more reason go reprove
The amorous Magnet which the North doth love.
Or preach divorce and say it is amisse
That with tall Elms the twining Vines should kisse
Then chide two such so fit, so equall faire   75
That in the world they have no other paire.
Whom it might seeme that Heaven did create
To restore man unto his first estate.
Yet she for honours tyrannous respect
Her own desires did and his neglect.   80
And like the Modest Plant at every touch
Shrunk in her leaves and feard it was too much.
    But who can paint the torments and that pain
Which he profest and now she could not faigne?

He like the Sun but overcast and pale: 85
Shee like a Rainbow, that ere long must faile,
Whose rosiall cheek where Heaven it selfe did view
Begins to separate and dissolve to dew.

  At last he leave obtaines though sad and slow,
First of her and then of himselfe to goe.   90
How comely and how terrible he sits
At once and Warre as well as Love befits!
Ride where thou wilt and bold adventures find:
But all the Ladies are got up behind.
Guard them, though not thy selfe: for in thy death
Th' Eleven thousand Virgins lost their breath.   96

  So *Hector* issuing from the Trojan wall
The sad *Iliades* to the Gods did call
With hands displayed and with dishevell' haire
That they the Empire in his life would spare.   100
While he secure through all the field doth spy
Achilles for *Achilles* only cry.
Ah ignorant that yet e're night he must
Be drawn by him inglorious through the dust.

  Such fell young *Villiers* in the chearfull heat   105
Of youth: his locks intangled all with sweat
And those eyes which the Sentinell did keep
Of love closed up in an eternall sleep.
While *Venus* of *Adonis* thinks no more
Slaine by the harsh tuske of the Savage Boare.   110
Hither she runns and hath him hurried farre
Out of the noise and blood, and killing warre:
Where in her Gardens of Sweet myrtle laid,
She kisses him in the immortall shade,

  Yet dyed he not revengelesse: Much he did   115
Ere he could suffer. A whole Pyramid
Of Vulgar bodies he erected high:
Scorning without a Sepulcher to dye.
And with his steele which did whole troops divide
He cut his Epitaph on either Side.   120

Till finding nothing to his courage fit
He rid up last to death and conquer'd it.
    Such are the Obsequies to *Francis* own:
He best the pompe of his owne death have showne.
And we hereafter to his honour will   125
Not write so many, but so many kill.
Till the whole Army by just vengeance come
To be at once his Trophee and his Tombe.

NOTES
INDEX OF FIRST LINES

NOTES

M.L.R. = Modern Language Review.
P M.L.A. = The Publications of the Modern Language Association (America).
T.L.S. = The Times Literary Supplement.

Page 1. *A Dialogue, Between the Resolved Soul, and Created Pleasure.*

ll. 21–22 'The Syberite myth, variously told of one who could not recline in full comfort on his downy couch because of the roughness of a single chance-fallen rose-leaf thereon', Grosart.

l. 51 soft] MS. Eng. poet d. 49 and Margoliouth.

l. 71 Centre] the centre of the Earth. [cos Fo.

Page 6. *On a Drop of Dew.* For a commentary on the relation between this poem and the Latin version which follows it, and between *The Garden* and *Hortus*, see Sir Herbert Grierson's *Metaphysical Lyrics and Poems of the Seventeenth Century* (1921). Margoliouth quotes Grierson's note which includes the observation that 'a careful reading suggests that the Latin in each case was written first and served as a guide rather than a text for the beautiful English verses'.

l. 23 blossoms green] Margoliouth records that Marvell uses the word 'green' twenty-five times in the 1681 folio.

l. 24 recollecting] collecting again.

l. 29 World excluding round] Margoliouth gives the paraphrase 'thus shutting out the world on every side'.

Page 9. *The Coronet.* Professor Legouis contrasts what he considers the puritanism of this piece with George Herbert's *Easter*.

l. 7 Towers] a high head-dress worn by women *O.E.D.*

l. 22 curious frame] elaborate frame of flowers.

Page 10. *Eyes and Tears.* There is a manuscript copy of this poem in the Bodleian (Tanner 306, f. 388): it has no particular value.

l. 35 *Cynthia* Teeming] a reference to the growing or full moon.

l. 38 its] the folio has 'it': this is just possible, but is more likely to be a misprint.

Page 12. *Bermudas.* The Bermudas were in people's minds. Marvell had lived at Eton in the house of the Rev. John Oxenbridge. Probably Legouis (pp. 182–3) is right in suggesting that the idea of the poem was the outcome of conversations between Marvell and Oxenbridge who had embarked for the Bermudas in 1635 because of the persecutions of Laud. Legouis refers to J. H. Lefroy's *Memorials of the Discovery and Early Settlement of the Bermudas or Somers Islands 1515–1685* (1877). See also Henry Wilkinson's *The Adventurers of Bermuda* (1933). The islands took their name from Sir G. Somers, who was wrecked upon them in 1609.

Margoliouth quotes from Captain John Smith's *The Generall Historie of Virginia, New England and the Summer Isles* (1624). In his notes to the Muses Library *Waller*, Thorn Drury refers the reader to Fairfax's *Godfrey of Bulloigne*, xv. 35–6; xvi. 11, and *The Faerie Queene*, iii. 6. 42. Waller writes of:

> That happy island where huge lemons grow
> And orange trees, which golden fruit do bear.

l. 20 *Ormus*] Hormuz, on the Persian Gulf.

l. 23 Apples] Pineapples.

l. 28 Ambergris] cf. 'The Gallery' l. 38: a fatty substance with a fragrant musky odour excreted by the sperm whale.

Page 14. *Clorinda and Damon.*

ll. 3–4 Scutcheon and blazons] terms used in heraldry.

l. 8 vade: Latin *vadere* to pass away.

Page 15. *A Dialogue between the Soul and Body.*

l. 14 This line is characteristic of Marvell. 'After he was stretch'd to such an height in his own fancy, that he could not look down from top to toe but his Eyes dazled at the Precipice of his Stature', *The Rehearsal Transpros'd* (1672), p. 64.

Page 16. *The Nymph complains for the death of her Faun.*

l. 17 *Deodands*] a personal chattel which having been the cause of a persons death was forfeited to the Crown. 'Scroope afterwards wrote to me for my pistols to shoot himself; but I declined lending them on the plea that they would be forfeited as a deodand', *Conversations of Lord Byron.*

ll. 99–100 *Heliades*] the three sisters of Phaeton so called of Helios (the Sun) their father.

> No lesse th' *Heliades* lament; who shead
> From drowned eyes vaine offerings to the dead;
> > *Ovid's Metamorphosis Englished by*
> > *George Sandys* (1626).

The Heliades were transformed into willow trees: their tears became amber.

Page 21. *To his Coy Mistress.*

l. 29 dust] Cooke: durst Fo.

l. 34 The word in the Fo. is 'glew'. Cooke emended this to 'dew', and this is the happiest solution of this famous crux. The word 'glew' is used in its modern sense in l. 16 of *Daphnis and Chloe.*

> Sudden Parting closer glews.

Margoliouth conjectured 'lew' (warmth): this is ingenious, possible, and involves the lesser alteration.

I have his authority for saying that he would not now contend for 'lew'. MS. Eng. poet. d. 49 Substitutes 'glew' for 'hew' in l. 33, and 'dew' for 'glew' in l. 34. Notwithstanding the unnecessary change made in l. 33, the MS. correction is of some weight. It, at least, shows that difficulty was felt about these two lines.

Page 23. *The Unfortunate Lover*. This poem hardly lends itself to a general note. As Professor Legouis wrote 'l'hyperbole est poussée si haut qu'un homme d'aujourd'hui est tenté d'y voir une intention de parodie'. The allusions in it are obscure. In *Andrew Marvell* (1940) there is a note (p. 29) in which it is said that this poem 'in particular recalls the series of emblems showing the lover's torments in Otto van Veen's *Amorum Emblemata* (Antwerp, 1608). The authors refer the reader to Professor Mario Praz's *Studies in Seventeenth Century Imagery* (1939). For the most part writers on Marvell have made little reference to the poem.

l. 36 bill] peck *O.E.D.*

l. 44 At sharp] with sharpened weapons Aitken.

l. 48 Ajax] 'On his return from Troy his vessel was wrecked on the Whirling Rocks, but he himself escaped upon a rock through the assistance of Poseidon and would have been saved in spite of Athena, but he used presumptuous words, and said he would escape the dangers of the sea in defiance of the immortals ... Ajax was swallowed up by the sea', Smith, *Odyssey* iv.

l. 57 *Banneret*] a knight made so on the battlefield.

l. 64 a red lover in a black field Aitken.

Page 25. *The Gallery*.

l. 5 *Arras*] was, of course, famous for its tapestries.

l. 11 Examining] testing *O.E.D.*

l. 18 *Aurora*] or *Eos*, goddess of the morning.

l. 35 *Halcyons* 'while the bird *alcyon* was breeding, there always prevailed calms at sea', Smith.

l. 42 do] MS. Eng. poet. d. 49 and Cooke: dost Fo.

l. 48 This line refers to the collections of Charles I and the Gonzagas, Dukes of Mantua.

Page 28. *Mourning.*

ll. 3–4 Grosart and Margoliouth quote 'to speculate his own Baby in their Eyes' from *The Rehearsal Transpros'd*, p. 66. The latter quotes from 'Weeping' in Cowley's *The Mistress*. This supports the view that infants are here reflections, not simply tears, as Aitken thought. It is difficult to be certain.

l. 20 *Danae* and the showr] Jupiter visited Danae in the form of a golden shower, and by him she became the mother of Perseus.

Page 30. *Daphnis and Chloe.*

l. 78 Gourmand *Hebrew*] more than one reference seems possible, that to Numbers xi seems the most appropriate.

l. 79 with] Cook: he Fo: l. 80. He] Cooke and] Fo. The corrections in these two lines have been accepted by subsequent editors.

Stanza XXI. The reproduction of ferns was not then understood. There are many references to their invisible seeds: they could be gathered at Midsummer midnight, when they made the gatherer himself invisible. Grosart refers to 'Staffordshire and American Folk-Lore', *N. and Q.* (4th Series, vii, p. 91): See also *1 Henry IV*, II. i., quoted by Margoliouth.

l. 88 The alternative of 'Scent' in MS. Eng. poet. d. 49 to 'Sent' of the Fo. is convenient.

Page 34. *The Definition of Love.*

l. 24 *Planisphere* here means an astrolabe.

Page 36. *The Picture of little T. C. in a Prospect of*

Flowers. Margoliouth suggests that T. C. was possibly Theophila Cornewall, the youngest daughter of William and Bridget Skinner, see 'Andrew Marvell: Some Biographical Points', *M.L.R.*, Oct. 1922.

Page 37. *Tom May's Death*. Thomas May who was born in 1595 died on the 13th November 1650. He is remembered as the translator of Lucan's *Pharsalia* (1627). He joined the parliamentary party and wrote *The History of the Parliament of England* (1647). 'He stood candidate for the laurell after B. Jonson; but Sir William Davenant carried it', Aubrey. Buried in Westminster Abbey, his body was taken up in September 1661. In the *Biographia Britannica* the present satire is said, on the evidence of ll. 85–90, to have been written after the Restoration on the ground that it refers to the exhumation.

l. 1. May 'came of his death after drinking with his chin tyed with his cap (being fatt): suffocated', Aubrey.

l. 6 Stevens Alley] or Canon row Stow's *Survey* (1603, Everyman edn.). May 'lodged in the little [court?] by Canon-rowe, as you goe through the alley', Aubrey.

l. 6 Grass?] Cooke: Grass Fo.

l. 10 *Ares*] possibly a tavern-keeper. Aitken suggested the pilot Ayres mentioned by Pepys in a letter of 8th May 1682.

l. 13 Ben Jonson died on the 6th of August 1637.

l. 18 *Brutus* and *Cassius*] Margoliouth believes, no doubt rightly, that the allusion is to the last Canto of Dante's *Inferno*:

Of th' other two

Whose heads are under, from the murky jaw
Who hangs, is Brutus: lo! how he doth writhe
And speaks not. The other, Cassius, that appears
  so large of limb.

See notes to Cary's *Dante*.

l. 21 *Emathian*] Cooke: *Emilthian* Fo.

> 'Warres more than civill in Æmathian plaines'
> l. 1 of May's *Lucan*

l. 26 translated [by Death] a pun.

l. 29 friend] Ben Jonson, 'To my chosen Friend...
Thomas May', verses before May's *Lucan*.

l. 38 *Pembroke* at the Masque] Philip Herbert, Earl of
Pembroke at a Masque in 1634 broke his staff over
May's shoulders, not knowing who he was, *Letters
and Despatches of Thomas Earl of Stafford*, 1740, i.
207.

l. 41 *Polydore*] Vergil (1470?–1555?), a native of
Urbino, who came to England in 1505: he was
Archdeacon of Wells and wrote *Historia Anglica*.
   Allan] one of the Alani:

> Unquiet Alans to the Caspian straight
> May's *Lucan*, viii. 223

l. 48–9 May was fond of parallels from Roman history.

l. 50 'The Santa Casa of Loreto is venerated as the
house of the Virgin, miraculously conveyed from
Nazareth (not from Bethlehem) to Illyria in 1291,
and finally to its present site', Margoliouth.

l. 56 May is accused of malice in *The Great Assises
Holden in Parnassus* (1645).

l. 62 Basket] Margoliouth suggests this may refer to
borsa, which received the votes in Florentine elec-
tions.

l. 68 World's] Cooke: World Fo.

l. 74 *Spartacus*] 'After praising Essex in the *History
of the Long Parliament of England*, May went over to
the Independents; and in the *Breviary of the History
of the Parliament of England* (1650) lauded Fairfax,
Cromwell, the New Model Army, and the Independent party ... Spartacus may refer to either

Essex or Fairfax or to the Parliamentary armies in general', Aitken. Spartacus was the chosen leader of a number of runaway slaves.

l. 82 The Council voted £100 for May's burial in Westminster Abbey.

l. 88 Eagles Plumes] Margoliouth quotes Du Bartas:

And so the Princely Eagles ravening plumes
The feathers of all other Fowls consumes.

l. 90 *Phlegeton*] the flaming river in the lower world.

l. 92 *Megæra*] also called *Erinyes*, represented as winged goddesses of terrible appearance with snakes entwined in their hair, bearing torches and scourges.

Page 42. *The Mower against Gardens.*

ll. 15–16 These lines refer to the Dutch mania for tulips. This was at its height between the years 1634 and 1637. For a good account of the mania see Wilfred Blunt's *Tulipomania* (Penguin Books, 1950).

l. 18 *Marvel of Peru*] called by Parkinson (1629) *Mirabilia Peruviana*. Robinson in *The English Flower Garden* says the most familiar species is *M. Jalapa*. Possibly its name appealed more to the poet than the plant does to the horticulturist.

ll. 29–30 Mr. John Gilmour tells me that these lines (which previous editors have been unable to explain) only refer 'to the practice of vegetative or asexual propagation of cherries and other fruits by budding and grafting which has, of course, been extensively practised for many hundred of years'.

Page 43. *Damon the Mower.*

l. 12 hamstring'd] lamed.

l. 21 made the Dog] mads the Dog MS. Eng. poet. d. 49. This is a possible, and even probable reading.

l. 83 Shepherds-purse] *Capsella Bursa-pastoris*, a common weed. Clowns-all-heal] The Marsh Woundwort. Both are supposed to stop bleeding, see Gerarde's *Herball* (1633), pp. 276 and 1004–5.

Page 50. *Musicks Empire*.

l. 5 *Jubal*] 'the father of all that play on the harpe and organs' Genesis (Geneva version)

> What passion cannot Music raise and quell!
> When Jubal struck the corded shell,
>
> Dryden

l. 6 tuned] Cooke: tun'd Fo.

Page 51. *The Garden*

l. 2 Oke] see note to l. 12 of 'To . . . Lovelace'.

l. 23 your] Cooke: you Fo.

ll. 27–32 The story of the metamorphosis of *Daphne* into a laurel, and *Syrinx* into a reed would have been familiar from Sandys' *Ovid* to those who did not know the Classics.

ll. 43–4 See Sir T. Browne's *Pseudodoxia Epidemica* (1646). One of the 'Vulgar Errors' was 'That all Animals of the Land, are in their kinde in the Sea.'

ll. 47–8 The exact meaning—if such can be expected —of these lines has been frequently discussed. The reader who is troubled by them must consult *inter alia* William Empson's *Some Versions of Pastoral*.

l. 66 Grosart and Aitken refer to Mrs. Hemans' Dial of Flowers and Charlotte Smith's Horologe of the Field. Linnæus formed a dial of forty-six flowers.

Page 57. *Fleckno, an English Priest at Rome*. Richard Flecknoe, immortalized by Dryden in *Mac Flecknoe*, was the butt of Marvell and Dryden for no very obvious reason. Flecknoe wrote a number of small books which, if not important, are not without interest. He was in Rome from 1645 to 1647. See his *Relation of ten years Travells in Europe, Asia, Affrique and America* (c. 1654). As Margoliouth notes,

Flecknoe describes himself as living a 'so melancholy a life, my Lute being silenc't and I never appearing in the *Park* but like a walking ghost, or a body without a soul'. In the *T.L.S.* for the 5th June 1924 (following an article in the *M.L.R.* for October 1922), Margoliouth gave the dates of Flecknoe's visits to the English College in Rome. He also suggested that Marvell was acting as tutor to an Edward Skinner.

l. 3 *Melchizedeck*] King of Salem and Priest of the most high God (Gen. xiv. 18) is a type of Christ (Heb. vii.) foretelling him. Marvell probably takes him as having a triple property as Prophet, Priest and King. Flecknoe's triple role of Priest, Poet and Musician may have recalled this.

l. 4 *Lord Brooke*] Fulke Greville. Flecknoe dedicated *The Affections of a Pious Soule* (1640) to Lady Nevill Brooke.

l. 12 Seeling ... sheet] the passage is punning on the properties of the 'coffin and of the room. Seeling can mean wall-hangings; ... sheet stands for a bed sheet and a winding-sheet', Margoliouth.

l. 18 *Stanza's*] appartment.

l. 57 Wright inserted 'the' before dinner: 'the' is not in the Fo.: MS. Eng. poet. d. 49 has 'our'.

l. 74 *Sotana*] cassock.

l. 76 Counsel of *Antioch*] There were several. The most famous was held in the year 341.

l. 98 Delightful] delighted.

l. 104 By] MS. Eng. poet. d. 49: Cooke: But Fo.

l. 126 *Nero's* Poem] 'All the while hee was singing, Lawfull it was not for anye person to depart out of the Theatre, were the cause never so necessarie', P. Holland's *Suetonius* (1606). A translation of *The History of the Twelve Cæsars* (1677) has been ascribed to Marvell on doubtful evidence.

l. 133 pilled] peeled.

l. 137 *Chancres* and *Poulains*] signs of diseases, chiefly venereal: *Poulain* a botch on the groine, Cotgrave.

l. 152 *Perillus*] a sculptor: he was the maker of the bronze bull of the tyrant Phalaris. Perillus is said to have been one of the victims of his own handiwork, Smith.

l. 158 t'was] Grosart: was Fo.

Page 63. *To his worthy Friend Doctor Witty.* The Latin and English poems to Dr. Witty were printed in *Popular Errors. Or the Errours of the People in Psysick First written in Latine by the learned Physitian James Primrose* ... (London, 1651). The original, *De Vulgi in Medicinâ Erroribus Libri quatuor*, was published in 1638.

Both Primrose and Witty were doctors at Hull: Witty had been an usher at the Hull Grammar School 1636–42. Marvell's remarks on the functions of translators are often overlooked. The poem is really an essay in criticism: it was not included in Spingann's *Critical Essays of the Seventeenth Century.* Margoliouth (ii, 348) prints part of a letter from Witty dated 29th August 1678: 'If there be anything now upon the loss of our dear friend Mr. M. for whom I am a sincere mourner ... you know where you may command.'

l. 17 *Cælia*] Margoliouth notes: probably Mary Fairfax, see ll. 707–8 of *Appleton House*:

> *She* counts her Beauty to converse
> In all the Languages as *hers*;

Page 64. *On Mr. Milton's Paradise Lost.* These verses were printed at the beginning of the second edition of *Paradise Lost* (1674), entered in the *Term Catalogue* for the 6th of July of that year. I have printed the text as given in the Folio of 1681. There are many variants, but they are of little importance,

and I have not recorded them. Two errors in the
Folio have been corrected: l. 33 has 'treats' and
l. 45 has 'might': *P.L.* (1674) has 'treatst' and
'mightst'. The attack on Dryden in the verses may
have been in part due to the hostility existing between Marvell and Dryden. In the famous dispute
between Samuel Parker and Marvell Milton's name
had been dragged in. Marvell had attacked Parker
in *The Rehearsal Transpros'd* (1672). In Parker's
reply, *A Reproof to the Rehearsal Transprosed*
(1673), he had referred to 'the writings of *J.M.* in
defence of the Rebellion and the Murther of the
King'. Marvell ridiculed Parker and defended
Milton in *The Rehearsal Transpros'd: The Second
Part* (1673). Although Dryden appreciated *Paradise
Lost*; and in the 'Apology for Heroick Poetry and
Poetic Licence', prefixed to *The State of Innocence*,
calls Milton's poem 'undoubtedly one of the greatest, most noble, and most sublime Poems, which
either this Age or Nation has produc'd', Marvell
probably disliked Dryden's treatment of Milton's
blank verse. *The State of Innocence* was not published till 1677, but copies of the Opera had got
about early in 1674, and Marvell may have heard
from Milton that he had given Dryden leave 'to
tagge his verses' (Aubrey's *Brief Lives* under Milton).
In the preface to *Religio Laici* (1682) Dryden calls
Marvell 'the Martin Mar-prelate of these times ...
the first Presbyterian scribbler who sanctified libels
and scurrility to the use of the good old cause'.
Political feeling was very high at this time, and
Dryden was probably referring to Marvell's satires,
chiefly circulated in manuscript, not to the present
verses.

l. 9. *Samson Agonistes* had been published with *Paradise Regained* in 1671.

l. 18 some less skilful hand] Aubrey writes that Mil-

ton's 'familiar learned acquaintance were Mr.
Andrew Marvell ... John Dreyden, esq. Poet
Laureate, who very much admires him, and went to
him to have leave to putt his Paradise Lost into a
drama in rhymne. Mr. Milton received him civilly,
and told him he would give him leave to tagge his
verses'.

l. 39 A reference to the belief that Birds of Paradise
had no feet and were therefor always on the wing.

l. 43 *Tiresias*]

> Blind *Thamyris* and blind *Maeonides*,
> And *Tiresias* and *Phineus*, Prophets old.
> *P.L.*, iii. 35–6

l. 47 *Town-Bays*] Bayes was the common nick-name
for Dryden: it originated in *The Rehearsal* (1672).
spells] I don't know what this means. Margoliouth
suggests 'does things by spells or stages'.

l. 49 bushy Points] for fastening hose. As can be seen
from contemporary prints, they were often tasselled.

l. 54 *Rhime*] a subject much under discussion, particularly by Dryden for the drama.

Page 69. The epitaphs on John Trott and Edmund
Trott (p. 73) were no doubt printed from manuscripts left by Marvell. They were written for tablets
in Laverstoke in Hampshire. The tablets are on the
north wall of the chancel of the old church. Margoliouth prints the corrections from the tablets themselves. I give the same versions. Margoliouth prints
the epitaphs of Sir John Trott and his parents. Sir
John Trott's may possibly have also been by Marvell.
They are in prose, and will be found on pages 262–3
of Margoliouth, Vol. I.

Page 70. *To Sir John Trott*. Margoliouth prints this
letter in vol. II of his edition with a note that John
Trott of Laverstoke in Hampshire was cr ted a

baronet October 12, 1660, and was M.P. for Andover till his death in 1672. He had two sons, John and Edmund, who both matriculated at Oriel College, Oxford, in 1660. 'Jonn died of smallpox before August 11, 1667, the date of Edmund's death of the same disease. This letter was written shortly after the "second shock" of Edmund's death and may, therefore, be dated towards the end of August 1667. It was the covering letter for the latin epitaph' on p. 76.

Page 76. *Upon the Hill and Grove at Bill-borow.* Thomas, 3rd Lord Fairfax, commander-in-chief for a time of the Parliamentary Army, was born at Denton in Wharfdale on the 17th January 1612, and died at Nunappleton on the 12th November 1671. A full account of him is given in *A Life of the Great Lord Fairfax* by Clements R. Markham (1870). Fairfax was fond of the Manor House at Bilborough. 'On Bilbrough Hill, 145 feet above the sea, there was then a great clump of trees which was a landmark for ships going up the Humber, the land rising very gradually from the Wharfe at Nunappleton, and being crowned by this conical grassy hill, with its leafy tuft', Markham. Francis Drake's *York* (1736) was Markham's authority for the statement that the Hill served as a landmark for ships going up the Humber, but, as Margoliouth says, Drake's statement may have had its source in Marvell's poem. Drake, however, writes 'a plump of trees upon it may be seen at forty miles distance'.

l. 11 hook-shoulder'd] the Fairfax property was near enough to the hills of the West Riding for Marvell to have acquired a personal distaste for 'mountains'.

l. 34 Plump] see above: Plum Fo.

l. 43 *Vera*] Fairfax married Anne Vere, daughter of Sir Horace Vere in 1637.

l. **73 ye**] MS. Eng. Poet d. 49, Grosart and subsequent editors: the Fo. has 'the', but 'ye' and 'the' are often alike in a seventeenth-century manuscript.

l. **74** *Oracles* in Oak] Dodona's Grove. Zeus gave his responses from lofty trees, Smith.

Page 79. *Upon Appleton House, to my Lord Fairfax.* The houses referred to in the last poem and in this were the seats of the Fairfax family. Appleton House was eight miles south of York: Bishop's Hill, where Mary Fairfax was born, was in York itself: Denton and Bilborough have been mentioned already. Not far from Denton was Fewston, where Fairfax's uncle, Edward Fairfax, the translator of Tasso, lived. Bishop's Hill with Denton and Ashwith came to the Fairfaxs as part of the inheritance of Isabella Thwaites. 'The Cistercian nunnery of Appleton, four miles from Steeton [Nun Appleton is south of Appleton Roebuck], was presided over in the time of the second Sir William Fairfax by the Lady Anna Langton. A young lady named Isabella Thwaites, who had been placed under her charge, met and became attached to William Fairfax; but the Abbess, who had other views for her ward, shut her up to prevent her meeting her lover. At length higher authorities interfered, and after a forcible entry into the nunnery, Isabella was released and married to Fairfax at Bolton Percy in 1518. She brought her husband the estates of Denton with Ashwith in Wharfdale and other property in York. ... In 1542 the Abbess, Anna Langton, by the irony of fate had to surrender her nunnery to Thomas and Guy, sons of the lady whom she had imprisoned. They pulled down the religious buildings, and built a house out of some of the materials', Aitken based on Markham.

Nun Appleton House, the subject of this poem was begun about 1637 and finished in 1650. 'It was a picturesque brick mansion with stone copings and a high steep roof, and consisted of a centre and two wings at right angles, forming three sides of a square facing the north ... The central part of the house was surmounted by a cupola, and clustering chimneys rose over the two wings. A noble park, with splendid oak trees, and containing 300 head of deer, stretched away to the north; while on the south side were the ruins of the old nunnery, the flower garden and the low meadows, called *ings*, extended to the banks of the Wharfe', Markham.

l. 6 vault] 'The bulk of the unborn scheme stretches the architect's brain till his skull serves for a model', Margoliouth.

l. 22 Mote] MS. Eng. Poet. d. 49, Wright and Margoliouth: Cooke and Aitken print Mole: Fo. has Mose.

l. 30 loop] as in a loop-hole.

l. 40 *Romulus* his Bee-like Cell] probably Grosart is right in saying that the *casa Romuli* of tradition suggested to Marvell's mind a covering holding its inhabitants as the waxen cell does the newly hatched bee.

l. 46 The *Circle* in the *Quadrature*!] constant references occur to this problem in the seventeenth century: but how far its nature was understood except by professional mathematicians is uncertain.

l. 64 invent] find out.

l. 65 *Frontispice of Poor*:] All that is known of Fairfax suggests that he was good to humble people as well as to his many friends who lived near Nun-Appleton.

l. 71 Markham and Margoliouth quote some lines by Fairfax (Bodl. MS. Fairfax 40):

Upon the New-built House att Appleton

beginning

> Think not ô Man that dwells herein
> This House's a stay but as an Inne.

l. 79 I have printed 'shady' of MS. Eng. Poet. d. 49 instead of 'shaddy' of the Fo.

l. 105 white] the Cistercian habit.

ll. 141–2 Crown] Margoliouth annotates 'perhaps of Angels', cf. Chapman's *Iliad* xv. 7.

l. 152 *Devoto*] 'devout, devoted, religious', Florio's *New World of Words* (1611).

ll. 179–80 'we lay in ambergris for the altar-cloths', Margoliouth.

l. 181 griv'd] grive obsolete form of grieve hurt or harm.

l. 221 state] estate.

l. 232 William Fairfax, a judge of the Common Pleas. He built a castle at Steeton, and died in 1495 Aitken.

ll. 241–4 It is uncertain to which of the Fairfaxes these lines apply; possibly Sir Thomas Fairfax, son of Sir W. Fairfax and Isabella Thwaites is meant. Grosart and others thought ll. 281–2 refer to the General himself. Milton's sonnet:

> Fairfax, whose name in arms through Europe rings

is not really evidence of this.

l. 245 Grosart has a note on this line which does not explain it.

l. 252 *Holy-Water Brush*] a brush used to sprinkle Holy Water *O.E.D.*

l. 253 disjointed] disturbed *O.E.D.*, distracted is what is meant here. Grosart has a characteristic conjecture that she 'was tottering through rheumatism'.

l. 274 Escheat] a legal term: the land reverted to the lord when the tenant died without a successor qualified to inherit.

l. 282 see note to ll. 241–4.

l. 292 *Dian*] French diane, the reveillé.

l. 295 Pan] of the musket-lock.

l. 320 nor] Cooke: or Fo. and Margoliouth.

l. 328 The wast] thee waste Aitken.

l. 336 *Switzers*] the Swiss guard at the Vatican have a black, yellow and red uniform.

l. 349 *Cinque Ports*] Fairfax was never Lord Warden; and the Cinque Ports are somewhat dragged in by way of contrast to the 'five imaginary Forts'.

ll. 357-8 A reference to the sensitive plant.

l. 363 *Cawwood castle*] at one time a seat of the Archbishops of York, was a few miles south of Nun-Appleton.

l. 380. Margoliouth explains this line as: 'whether he is going downwards or forwards'.

l. 385 scene ... Engines strange] a reference to the contrivances used in the performances of elaborate Masques.

l. 395 *Rail*] the corncrake.

l. 402 Cates] provisions here: also dainties *O.E.D.*

l. 416 *Sourdaine*] 'a little pipe put in the mouth of a Trumpet, to make it sound low', Cotgrave.

l. 426 Hay] as the Hay is a dance there may be some play in the word intended.

l. 428 *Alexander's Sweat*] Alexander's skin 'had a marvellous good savour', North's *Plutarch*.

l. 437 *Desert Memphis Sand*] Memphis, a city of Egypt about 10 miles above the Pyramids.

l. 439 *Roman Camps*] really the tumuli of earlier date.

l. 444 Lilly] although Cooke states that Lilly was a cloth dyer: Margoliouth, no doubt correctly, identifies him as Sir Peter Lely.

l. 446 rase] *tabula rasa.*

l. 447 Marvell visited Spain. In the letter from Milton to Bradshaw, referred to in the introduction, Milton wrote 'he [Marvell] spent foure years abroad in Holland, France, Italy, and Spaine'.

l. 454 *Beast*] MS. Eng. Poet. d. 49: Cooke: Breast Fo.

ll. 455-6 Davenant's *Gondibert* (1651), II, vi. 60:

Then strait a universal Heard appears.

Stanza LX. This unnatural natural history is a little confused. Coleridge recorded that experiments in the apparent life of a wetted horsehair are 'common ... with schoolboys in Cumberland and Westmorland'. Leeches can cause trouble to horses and cattle when they drink from ponds.

l. 491 *Pedigrees*] here alludes to the branching shown in genealogical trees.

l. 493 Does this refer to the felling of trees which always occurs in a war?

l. 502 *Fifth Element*.] There were supposed to be four elements, earth, air, fire and water.

l. 508 *Corinthean Porticoes*] suggests the leafy colonnades of the wood.

l. 535 The Dutch believed that the stork left one of its young behind when leaving a house where she had built.

l. 537 *Hewel*] the green-wood pecker.

l. 538 *Holt-felsters*] woodcutters.

l. 580 *Mexique Paintings*] 'paintings' made of feathers. Grosart and Margoliouth refer to *Humane Industry* (1661).

l. 586 could ... hit] 'could provide me with a masquing habit suitable to my studies', Margoliouth.

l. 610 ye gadding *Vines*] cf. **Lycidas** 'the gadding vine'. Marvell sometimes echoes *Lycidas*. Milton's poem was published with other poems on the death of Edward King at Cambridge in 1638. *Justa Edouardo King* was a collection of academical verses, and so would almost certainly have been read by Marvell, who was at Trinity when the volume appeared.

l. 629 'your serpent of Egypt is bred now of your mud by the operation of your sun: so is your crocodile', *Anthony and Cleopatra*.

l. 636 slick] sleek. To polish *O.E.D.*

l. 640 *Narcissus* like] Narcissus fell in love with his own image reflected in a fountain.

l. 651 *young Maria*] Fairfax's daugher to whom Marvell was tutor.

l. 659 whisht] hushed.

l. 668 *Eben Shuts*] Ebony (black) shutters.

l. 669 *Halcyon*] here the kingfisher?

l. 753 *Thessalian Tempe's Seat*] a beautiful valley between Mounts Olympus and Ossa.

l. 755 *Arunjuez*] Aitken, on the Tagus: it had famous gardens: Arunjeuz Fo.

l. 756 *Bel-Retiro*] Buen Retiro, a royal residence near Madrid.

ll. 761–2 Aitken followed Cooke in printing these lines as:

> 'Tis not, as once appeared the world,
> A heap confused together hurled;

but there is no authority for the change; even the original is clearer.

Stanza LXXXXVII. Coracles or *Leathern Boats* are, or were not long ago, carried on fishermen's heads.

Page 107. *On the Victory obtained by Blake over the Spaniards* ... in ... 1657. This poem was first printed in *A New Collection of Poems and Songs. Written by several Persons, Collected by John Bulteel, Printed by J.C. for William Crook* ... (1674). This volume was re-issued with a cancel title-page as *Melpomene: Or the Muses Delight* ...

(1678). See A. E. Case's *Bibliography of English Poetical Miscellanies* (1935). There are many small variants between the text of 1674 and that printed in the folio of 1681. These are recorded by Margoliouth. The folio text, which is the better, is followed here. In the folio the poem is addressed to Cromwell, e.g. line 16 has 'are your Flags': the 1674 version has 'th' English Flags'.

Cruising off Cadiz, Admiral Blake (1599–1657) received news that a fleet from America had reached Santa Cruz, Teneriffe. He at once set sail, and arrived at Santa Cruz at daybreak on April 20, 1657. Entering the bay he found the West Indian fleet anchored round the shore, commanded by the castle and forts; but by the evening all the Spanish vessels were destroyed, without the loss of a single English vessel. The victory was celebrated by a public thanksgiving on June the 3rd; but Blake died on his way home, on August the 7th at the entrance of Plymouth Sound (see Hepworth Dixon's *Life of Blake*, pp. 346–54), Aitken.

l. 9 Intrails] 1674: Intails Fo.

l. 23 theirs] Aitken substituted 'it', i.e. the darkness, for 'theirs' of the Fo: but this is not necessary.

l. 59 Ore 1674 substituted for the reader's convenience; Oar Fo.

l. 98 An allusion to the Spanish Commandant's answer to the Dutch captain who wished to leave on learning of Blake's approach.

l. 117 *Stainer*] Sir Richard Stayner who captured the Plate fleet on September 8, 1656, Aitken. Cf. Waller's 'Of a war with Spain, and a fight at sea'. See G. Thorn-Drury's notes to the poem in The Muses' Library [1893].

l. 129 ne'r . . . aspire] 1674: never. . .a Spire Fo.

l. 132 its] i.e. the fire's Margoliouth.

Page 112. *A Dialogue between Thyrsis and Dorinda.* Grosart and Aitken made small emendations of the text as printed in the Fo. As Margoliouth says, the text of this poem is more corrupt than that of any other in the Fo.: it is also out of its place, between poems of quite a different kind. Margoliouth constructed a better text than that in the Fo. from two manuscripts. (B.M. Add. 29921 and Bodl. Rawl. poet 81).

Mr. J. B. Leishman found versions in *A Crew of Kind London Gossips* (1663): he then found the poem with music in John Gamble's *Ayres and Dialogues* (1659) and in *Choice Ayres* (1675) with music by Matthew Locke, and in two later volumes. I have found the poem in *New Court Songs and Poems By R.* [   ] *V.* [   ] *Gent.* (1672). It was evidently popular as a song. I have adopted Margoliouth's text with two changes. Line 34 in the 1659 version has 'cool' instead of 'cold' of the Fo. Margoliouth has *Carillo* for *Corellia* in l. 45. Mr. Leishman suggested that the name should be *Carillo* as this is found in *England's Helicon* (1600), see Mr. Margoliouth's letter to the *T.L.S.*, 19th May 1950, embodying Mr. Leishman's discoveries.

As *A Dialogue* is one of Marvell's less successful poems it has not seemed worth while to give textual notes, especially as some of the departures from the Fo. cannot be established. See *T.L.S.*, 8th August 1952, p. 517.

l. 28 Antidate] Antedate.

l. 33 consorts] here the word means singing in harmony. *Thyrsis* is here (as by Margoliouth) made to speak ll. 43–4. This follows the text of *New Court Songs*. The speaker's name was omitted in the Fo.

Page 114. *The Character of Holland.* War with the Dutch broke out in May 1652. Tromp anchored his fleet off Dover without saluting the castle. An ob-

stinately fought engagement followed, and the
Dutch were accused of treachery in attacking Blake's
fleet while negotiations for a treaty were pending
(Bisset's *Commonwealth of England*, ii. 313–29).
In August the hostile fleet met off the Shetland
Islands; but a storm occurred which did much more
damage to Tromp's ships than to Blake's. The description in the *Life of Van Tromp* agrees exactly
with Marvell's: 'Our sails were all rent and torn in
pieces, and the waves rolled through them ...
throwing their foam up to the very heaven' (Bisset,
ii, 343). On September 28 Blake engaged De Witt
and De Ruyter off the Thames. Next day the Dutch
fleet refused to renew the fight, and fled. On November 29, however, Tromp appeared in the Downs, and
on the following day, partly through a sudden
change in the wind, Blake was defeated off Dunge-
ness. Two of our ships were captured, one burnt
and three blown up. The wind, however, prevented
Tromp pursuing; but there is a tradition that he
carried a broom at his masthead [discredited by
Gardiner] to indicate that he had swept the English
from the Seas. Colonels Richard Deane and Monck
were then appointed generals of the fleet in association with Blake. Another battle occurred off Portland, February 18, 1653, when both sides suffered
severely and Blake was wounded. This was an English victory according to Masson's *Milton*, IV, 376–
7. In the next fight, on June 3, 1653, the Dutch
were defeated, but Deane fell early in the day by
Monck's side, see Aitken.

This satire on the Dutch was written early in
1653, presumably before the death of Deane, who
is mentioned in l. 150. As we claimed that the
Dutch should render obeisance ('vail', l. 107) to the
English Flag and pay tribute for fishing in the North
Sea Marvell's patriotism now seems somewhat ex-

cessive. He took a more reasonable view of affairs when he wrote *The Growth of Popery* (1678). One hundred lines of the poem were published in a folio by Robert Horn at the Angel in Pope's Head Alley, 1665. No copy of this edition is known, but the lines and imprint are given in *The Harleian Miscellany* (v. 613). An eight-line conclusion, not by Marvell, attempting to make the verses applicable to the War with the Dutch at the time of their publication —the war of Dryden's *Essay of Dramatick Poesie* —were added to this edition which was entered on the Stationers Register on the 13th of June 1665. The edition was reprinted in quarto by Horn in 1672 for the so-called second Dutch War. Aitken (ii, 124–5) was lent a copy by Buxton Forman. The poem was printed in full for the first time in the Fo.

l. 5 alluvion] matter deposited by flood or inundation *O.E.D.*: it is also a legal term for new land formed by the action of water.

l. 8 because of their drinking habits.

l. 26 *Mare Liberum*] a book by Grotius of this name. The English claimed that the Channel was 'the British sea': Selden's *Mare Clausum*, which attempts to refute Grotius, was published in 1632.

l. 28 *Level-coyl*] jouer à cul-levé, Cotgrave. Marvell means that the land and water strove to supplant one another. Ben Jonson in *A Tale of a Tub*, III. 5, uses the expression for a disturbance, see Herford and Simpson, *Ben Johnson, IX*.

l. 32 *Cabillau*] (French) codfish.

l. 36 *Duck* and *Drake*] the idle amusement of making flat stones skim along the water.

l. 49 *Dyke-grave*] an officer in charge of the sea walls. Margoliouth cites Howell's *Epistolæ Ho-Elianæ*, i. iv.

l. 53 *Half-anders*] a pun on Hol-anders.

l. 62 *Poor John*] dried hake, cf. *The Tempest*, II. ii. 28

l. 65 *Marg'ret*] This is presumably the lady whose monument Evelyn went to see from *The Hague* (*Diary*, 1 Sept. 1641). She was reputed to have had as many children at one birth as there are days in the year.

l. 78 *Village*] The Hague.

l. 80 *Hogs*] The States-General were addressed (in Dutch) as Hoog-mogenden. English satirists applied the phrase Hogans-mogans to Dutchmen in general. Cf. *Hogan-Moganides, or the Dutch Hudibras* (1674).

l. 82 *Civilis*] a chief among the Batavi.

l. 86 square wooden stoves containing charcoal or some such fuel were in use in churches at least as late as 1913 in the big cold churches in Holland.

l. 94 *Butter-coloss*] the nickname Butter box and such like was given to Dutchmen *O.E.D.*

l. 96 *Snick and Sneer*] a combat with knives. Johnson in his *Dictionary* quotes from Wiseman's *Surgery*, 'Among the Dunkirkers where *snick* and *sneer* was in fashion ...'

l. 98 *Athos*] Dinocrates proposed to represent Mount Athos in a human form, *Dict. of Classical Antiquities.*

l. 106 Western golden Sands] gold from America.

l. 114 *Burgomaster of the Sea*] Van Tromp.

l. 115 Brand wine] Brandy.

l. 120 *Case-Butter ... Bullet-cheese*] case or canister shot: *Bullet cheese*] spherical Dutch cheeses. Margoliouth comments 'Van Tromp sees no more result than if he had used butter for case shot and cheese for bullets'.

l. 124 Blake engaged Van Tromp on the 29th of November 1652 ... but had to seek shelter in English harbours.

l. 127 careen] the position of a ship heeled over on one side *O.E.D.*

l. 130 *Halcyon*] meaning a period of a fortnight's calm whilst the Halcyon brooded on her floating nest.

l. 135 *Bucentore*] Bucentaur, the State Barge of Venice.

l. 136 *Sea-Nuptials*] I suppose this is a reference to Venice wedding the Sea:

> And, when she took unto her herself a Mate,
> She must espouse the everlasting sea.
>
> Wordsworth

l. 137 now] Thompson: how Fo.

ll. 137–8 *Hydra of seaven Provinces ... Infant Hercules*] the new-born Commonwealth, which in its infancy strangled a Hydra, thus surpassing the elder hero, who only strangled two snakes in his cradle, and found the Hydra a task for his maturer years, Grosart. Margoliouth thinks the allusion is probably to the English victory off Portland Bill 18–20 February 1653.

l. 139 After all, the Dutch hydra was only a tortoise; its one neck had been cut by Blake, Margoliouth.

l. 150 See opening note.

l. 152 *Pluto*] Hades or Pluto, the God of the Nether World.

Page 118. *An Horation Ode upon Cromwel's Return from Ireland.* First printed in Thompson's edition of the *Works*. Although the authorship has never been seriously in doubt the ode was not definitely proved to be by Marvell until the copy of the Folio of 1681 (C. 59. i. 8) was discovered. As the poem is upon 'Cromwell's return from Ireland' which happened at the end of May 1650 and he went to Scotland at the end of July of the same year, it was probably written in June 1650. Margoliouth calls attention to correspondence in *The Times Literary Supplement*, 29th January 1920 *et seq.*, in which part of the ode is compared with Lucan's *Pharsalia*.

There are verbal parallels between the ode and the passage, in Book I of May's translation, beginning 'But restlesse valour'.

l. 2 now] this may refer to more than one period; but the most likely time is that when the poem was written.

ll. 13–20. These lines are obscure. Aitken suggested 'Restless Cromwell ... first broke his fiery way through his own party; for to ambition 'courage high' rivals and enemies are the same, and with ambitious men (such) to restrain their energies is more than to oppose them'.

l. 15 Side] party Aitken. An alternative meaning is suggested by Margoliouth: 'the lightning is conceived as tearing through the side of its own body the cloud'.

l. 15 thorough] Thompson: through Fo.

l. 24 'Of those things which growe out of the Earth, Lightning blasteth not the Laurell tree'
P. Holland's *Pliny*, 1601

l. 32 Bergamot] a kind of pear.

l. 38 antient Rights] cf. *Tom May's Death*, l. 69.

l. 42 penetration] *Nat. Philos.* Used for a supposed or conceived occupation of the same space by two bodies at the same time *O.E.D.*

ll. 47–52 Charles I fled from Hampton Court to Carisbrooke in November 1647; and it was often said, though without foundation, that Cromwell had connived at the escape for his own ends, Aitken. See Sir C. Firth's *Cromwell*, p. 185.

l. 52 case] plight M.E.; but probably here 'cage'.

l. 69 For when they digged there for the foundation of the said temple, and chaunced to find within the ground a man's head ...' P. Holland's *Pliny* (1601), Bk. 28, Chap. 2.

ll. 74 and 86 Cromwell was in Ireland from the 13th of August 1649 till May 1650, Firth's *Cromwell*.

l. 85 Commons] Thompson: *Common* Fo.

l. 106 *Party-coloured*] For the same pun on the deri-
vation of Pict from *pingere*, see Cleveland's *The
Rebel Scot:* 'You Picts in gentry and devotion',
Margoliouth.

l. 107 sad] steadfast.

ll. 117–18 The cross-hilt of the sword would avert the
Spirits of the shady Night.

Page 121. *The First Anniversary.* This poem was first
published in quarto in 1655 for Samuel Gellibrand.
It was one of the poems which were cancelled in
ordinary copies of the Fo. The text given here is
from C. 59. i. 8.

The poem appears in *Poems on Affairs of State,*
Vol. IV. (1707), and in *Poems on Several Occasions:
viz. Waller's Anniversary on the Government of the
Lord Protector* 1655 ... (1717). In the last two
volumes it is attributed to Waller, possibly, as
Margoliouth suggests, because Waller had published *A Panegyrick on Oliver Cromwell* in 1655.
Marvell's enemy, Samuel Parker, knew the piece
was by Marvell. 'At length, by the interest of *Milton,*
to whom he was somewhat agreeable for his ill-
natur'd wit, he was made Under-secretary to *Cromwell's* Secretary. Pleas'd with which honour, he
publish'd a congratulatory poem in praise of the
Tyrant; but when he had a long time labour'd to
squeeze out a panegyrick he brought forth a satyr
upon all rightfull Kings; saying that *Cromwell* was
the sun, but other Monarchs were slow bodies,
slower than *Saturn* in their revolutions, and darting
more hurtful rays upon the earth ...', *History of
His Own Time* (1727). This poem was one of those
Thompson included in his *Addenda.* His text contains some errors or different readings, which I have

not recorded. Aitken used, but did not always follow, the edition of 1655.

Cromwell was installed as Protector on the 16th of December 1653.

Margoliouth quotes freely by way of illustration, from Henry Fetcher's *The Perfect Politician* (1660).

l. 12 The Jewel of the yearly Ring] Cromwell's crest, a demi-lion rampant holding a ring was incorporated in the great Seal of the Protector, see Firth's *Cromwell*.

l. 16 *Saturn*] The revolution is 10,759 days. Uranus and Neptune had not been discovered.

l. 17 *Platonique*] P. year, a cycle in which the heavenly bodies were supposed to go through all their possible movements, and return to their original relative positions, see *O.E.D.*

l. 20 *China* clay] Chinese porcelain was believed to be made of earth which lay in preparation underground for a century, Aitken. Margoliouth refers to Sir T. Browne's *Pseudodoxia Epidemica* (1646), ii. 5, par. 7.

l. 23 some] is here singular.

Frontier Town] Grosart writes 'probably the reference is to some town to which Richelieu brought the king down, that he might be present after the toil of the siege was over'. Grosart's notes are sometimes wild: but I cannot explain the words.

l. 41 Image-like] i.e. like the clock figures striking the hour on a bell, Margoliouth.

l. 41 an] 1655: and Fo.

l. 44 wooden Heads] cf. *Love's Labour Lost*, v. ii. 600–2, Margoliouth.

ll. 47–8 These difficult lines are best explained by a passage in Burnet's *Shakespeare and Greek Philosophy* (1916). Only a portion of the note (given in full by Margoliouth) can be quoted here: 'the function of Music is to overcome the barrier [between the soul of man and the soul of the world] and it is able to do so because it is able to reach the soul. . .'

l. 49 *Amphion*] The son of Zeus. Hermes gave Amphion a lyre, and he thenceforth practised song and music whilst his twin brother Zethus hunted and tended the flocks. When Amphion played it is said that the stones moved of their own accord and formed a wall. There are many contemporary allusions, chiefly satirical, to Cromwell's fondness for music.

l. 60 joyning] Thompson: joying Fo.

l. 66 City of the seven gates] Thebes.

l. 68 Margoliouth quotes from Henry Fletcher's *The Perfect Politician*, 1660, p. 250: 'Because there can be no superstructure without a Basis, an *Instrument* was framed to be the foundation of the present Government.'

l. 69 hack] mangle *O.E.D.*

ll. 69–70 refer to earlier attempts made to form a constitution.

l. 90 Contignation] a joining or framing together of boards *O.E.D.*

l. 99 'The following fifty lines refer to Cromwell's attempt to form a general Protestant league, which the Dutch and Swedes, led by reasons of State, were unwilling to join', Aitken.

ll. 105–58 This passage is obscure unless the closest attention is given to it. Margoliouth explains that it takes its colour from the apocalyptic prophecies of the books of Daniel vii–viii and Revelations xii.–xx. Cromwell's government is greeted as a preparation for the final fulfilment of the *holy Oracles* (l. 108).

ll. 151–2 Cf. Milton's *Nativity Ode* (published in 1645):

Swindges the scaly Horrour of his foulded tail.

l. 161 Cromwell's mother died on the 16th November 1654 in her ninety-fourth year. When Cromwell took up his residence at Whitehall in April 1654 his mother removed with him, Firth.

ll. 171–2 The Levellers were particularly troublesome: they complained that the Revolution of 1648 had stopped too soon, and that the Republic was not an absolute democracy, Firth. There were also the Fifth Monarchy men, not to mention the Royalists.

l. 177 Cromwell's coach was overturned, when he himself was driving ['six great German Horses'] in Hyde Park, on September 29, 1654, Aitken; Thurloe's *State Papers*.

l. 184 purling] purl to embroider: 'purl' with silver', Sandy's *Ovid*.

Gold embroidery] cf. Hall, *Henry VIII*, an 12, cloth of tissue, and powdered with red roses, purled with fine gold', Aitken. Ore can also mean Lemster wool *O.E.D.*, but hardly here.

l. 203 Panique] of noise, etc., such as was attributed to Pan *O.E.D.*

l. 205 Center] see note to l. 71 of 'A Dialogue between the Resolved Soul . . .'

l. 215 The passages beginning with this line have biblical analogies and parallels more or less close to Marvell's poem. The poem was addressed to readers chiefly, no doubt, of the Puritan side, many of whom would have been quite familiar with the Old Testament and to whom the references would have been clear enough. Even as late as 1655 the Geneva, rather than the Authorized Version, would very likely have been much in use. The lines 215–20 only become intelligible if one turns to 2 Kings ii. 11–13, 'And as they went walking and talking, beholde there appeared a charet of fire and horses of fire, and did separate them twaine. So Elijah went up by a whirle winde into heaven. And Elisha saw it, and he cryed, My father, my father, the Charet of Israel and the horsemen therefor: and hee saw him no more: and he tooke his own clothes, and rent them in two pieces ...': and 1 Kings xviii. 44–6 'Behold there ariseth a little cloud out of the sea like a mans hand' ... and so on.

l. 249 'Gideon extended the war with the Midianites so as to include the people of Succoth and Penuel' (Judges viii.), Aitken. Margoliouth points to the parallel in Judges viii. and ix.

l. 269 baleful *Tritons*] monsters 'of semi-human form' *O.E.D.*

l. 270 Corposants] 'Marine meteors, which Portuguese marines call the Bodies of the Saints, *Corpos Santos*', Thompson. See the frontispiece to J. Livingston Lowes' *The Road to Xanadu* (1927), and his note on these lights in the sky.

l. 275 artless] unskilful *O.E.D.*

l. 283 eight] Cromwell, his wife, two sons and four daughters.

ll. 283–8 See Genesis ix. 20–1: 'And Noah began to be an husbandman, and he planted a Vineyard. And he dranke of the wine and was drunken.' The story of Noah's drunkenness figured very much more in legends and commentators than in the Bible itself.

l. 286 wouldst] 1655: would Fo.

l. 293 *Chammish*] like Ham (Vulgate, Cham) to 320 satirizes the religious sects of the time, especially the Fifth Monarchy men and the Quakers. Christopher Feake and Sydrach Simpson were both imprisoned for preaching sedition against Cromwell.

l. 308 Tulipant] Turban *O.E.D.*

l. 313 Munser] this may refer to Thomas Munzer, an Anabaptist, or to the dregs of Munster, the city captured by the Anabaptists.

l. 316 Points] for fastening hose.

l. 319 Some members of fanatical sects went naked.

l. 331 blacks] funeral hangings.

ll. 345–72 'Penn's expedition against the Spanish

colonies in the West Indies, which sailed in December 1654 is probably referred to here', Aitken. An expedition under Blake may also be partly the subject of these lines.

l. 352 their] Margoliouth: our Fo.

ll. 355–6

A Scot, when from the Gallows-Tree got loose
Drops into Stix and turns a Soland Goose.
Cleveland, *The Rebel Scot.*

There was a legend that leaves from a certain tree falling into the water became solan geese. This is probably connected with the well-known Barnacle tree, see Gerarde's *Herbal* (1633).

Page 133. *A Letter to Doctor Ingelo.* This poem is fully annotated by Margoliouth.

Bulstrode Whitelocke (1605–1675) remembered chiefly for his *Memorials of the English Affairs from the Reign of Charles I to the happy Restoration of King Charles II* (published in 1682), was Ambassador Extraordinary to Sweden in September 1653. He took Nathaniel Ingelo (1621?–83) with him as chaplain. Ingelo had been elected a Fellow of Eton in 1650. Marvell's residence at Eton began in July 1653. It was presumably at Eton that the two men met.

Page 138. *Two Songs at the Marriage of the Lord Fauconberg and the Lady Mary Cromwell.* Mary, Cromwell's third daughter, became on November 19, 1657, second wife of Thomas Belasyse (1627–1700), second Viscount Fauconberg, afterwards Earl of Fauconberg. She died in 1712. Lord Fauconberg went over to the Parliamentarians during Cromwell's rule, became a Royalist again at the Restoration, and joined in the invitation to William III to accept the English crown.

l. 30 *Anchises*] means Robert Rich, who had married on November 11, 1657, Cromwell's fourth daughter *D.N.B.*

Page 143. *A Poem upon the Death of O. C.* This was one of the poems which were cancelled in ordinary copies of the Fo. Even from C. 59. i. 8, ll. 185–324 are wanting, as these should have been printed on the last two leaves of the volume. For these lines Thompson's edition has hitherto been the only authority. MS. Eng. poet. d. 49 now ranks as the prime source of the text of these lines. As, however, Thompson appears to have had two sources before him I have allowed the lines as printed by Thompson to stand with some modifications. It is possible that Thompson made considerable use of MS. Eng. poet. d. 49. The title of the poem, as printed by Thompson, is the same as that given in MS. Eng. poet. d. 49, that is: 'A Poem upon the Death of His late Highness the Lord Protector'. See, however, notes to ll. 132, 201, 229 and 273. Line 275 in the manuscript has 'seate' in the place of 'state': l. 291 has (like Thompson) 'yet': probably Margoliouth's emendation 'at' is right. I have generally followed MS. Eng. poet. d. 49 in the matter of capitals; but I have deleted some exclamation marks, presumably introduced by Thompson. I have in places printed, 'ed' from MS. Eng. poet. d. 49 instead of Thompson's 'd'. I have printed proper names in italics to bring the text into typographical accord with that part of the poem which appears in C. 59. i. 8. The text in such minor matters is necessarily eclectic. Cromwell died on the 3rd of September 1658.

l. 30 Elizabeth, Lady Claypole, the Protector's favourite daughter died on the 6th of August 1658. 'The Protector was much with her in her last days', Firth.

l. 48 his growing] MS. Eng. poet. 49 and Thompson: her growing Fo.

l. 53 Limbs of wax] refers to the practice of melting a wax figure of an enemy: it was supposed to harm the living original.

l. 62 feigns] conceals.

l. 67 purple Locks] The allusion may be to the story of Nisus and Scylla. Nisus, King of Megara, was besieged by Minos. Scylla, daughter of Nisus, fell in love with Minos, and to win him cut off her father's famous lock of purple hair, on which his life depended. See Sandy's *Ovid*, Book viii:

This [a city] Nisus held; whose head a purple haire
'Mong those of honourable silver bare.

l. 78 A reference to a mirrour held before a dying person's mouth to ascertain if life is extinct.

ll. 79-80. These are common allusions to such unnatural natural history as the song of the dying swan and the Pelican feeding its young from its own breast.

l. 108 celebrates] MS. Eng. poet. d. 49, Thompson: celebrate Fo.

ll. 112 *et seq*. There was a great storm just before Cromwell died. There are contemporary allusions to his being carried away in a tempest, jocular in *Hudibras*:

Toss'd in a furious hurricane
Did Oliver give up his reign.

l. 121 lead] MS. Eng. poet. d. 49, Grosart: dead Fo.

ll. 126 *et seq*. There was an epidemic of low fever in the autumn of 1657, and again in the spring and summer of 1658, and a day of humiliation for it was fixed for May the 4th, 1658, Aitken quoting the *Cal. of State Papers Dom.*, 1657–8, pp. xli, 380. See Evelyn's *Diary*, 15th May 1658.

l. 132 This is the line as printed in C. 59. i. 8 and MS. Eng. poet. d. 49. Aitken, following Thompson, has:

The world with throes laboured beneath their load

l. 137 Margoliouth refers to Judges v. 20: 'the stars in their courses fought against Sisera'.

l. 144 The battles of Dunbar and Worcester were both fought on the 3rd of September in 1650 and 1651 respectively.

l. 154 In September 1658 a body of 2,000 Spanish foot and 1,500 horse under the Prince de Ligne was defeated on its march from Ypres to Tournay, and the greater part made prisoners by Turenne and the Anglo-French army, J. S. Clarke's *Life of James the Second* (1816) i. 366.

l. 162 'And he buried him in a valley in the land of Moab ..., but no man knoweth of his sepulchre unto this day', Deuteronomy xxxiv. 6.

ll. 173–4 The capture of Dunkirk from the Spaniards (1658) and of Jamaica (1655), Margoliouth.

l. 187 The Scotch, under the Duke of Hamilton, were defeated by Cromwell near Preston, on the 17th of August 1648.

l. 188 The surrender of Clonmell on 10th May 1650 was the last incident in Cromwell's Irish campaign.

l. 189 Lieut.-Colonel Roger Fenwick, who was mortally wounded at the battle of the Dunes, 4th June 1658.

l. 192 'So the Sunne abode in the mids of the heaven, and hasted not to go downe for a whole day', Joshua x. 13.

ll. 201–2 Cromwell's family owed its name and its fortune to Thomas Cromwell, Earl of Essex, the Minister of Henry VIII: 'I was by birth a gentleman living neither in any considerable height nor yet in obscurity', Firth, p. 1.

l. 201 dos claime] Margoliouth and MS. Eng. poet. d. 49: disclaime Thompson.

l. 215 cast] calculate.

l. 226 'And that to govern you is a task Heaven only could accomplish', Aitken.

l. 229 refuse] Wright and Margoliouth: reffuse MS. Eng. poet. d. 49: refuge Thompson.

l. 234 Janus's double gate of war and peace.

l. 242 'And David daunced before the Lorde with all his might, and was girded with a linen Ephod', 2 Samuel vi. 14.

l. 245 *Francisca*] Frances, Cromwell's youngest daughter.

l. 259 faigne] imagine.

l. 266 own plant]. the oak

l. 273 fall] MS. Eng. poet. d. 49, Grosart: full Thompson.

l. 275 state] Thompson: seate MS. Eng. poet. d. 49.

l. 291 at] Margoliouth: yet MS. Eng. poet. d. 49, Thompson.

l. 305 Richard Cromwell was proclaimed Protector on the day of his father's death. He lived till 1712.

Page 155. *To . . . Mr Richard Lovelace*. This is one of the commendatory poems at the beginning of Lovelace's *Lucasta* (1649).

l. 12 Civicke crowne] the crown was of oak leaves and was awarded for saving a citizen's life in battle. *Nettleship and Sandys* give an illustration.

l. 15 Caterpillar] rapacious persons of the state.

ll. 21–2 The Ordinance of Parliament of June 1643 against printing unlicensed books, which called forth Milton's *Areopagitica* (1644) was in force; in fact *Lucasta* was licensed on 4 February 1648, although not entered on the *Stationers' Register* till May 1649.

l. 22 grim consistory] court of presbyters.

l. 30 The famous song 'Tell me not (Sweet) I am un-
kinde'.

l. 31 For a full account of the Kentish petition 'that
the militia might not be otherwise exercised in that
county than the known law permitted, and that the
Book of Common Prayer established by law might
be observed' (Clarendon) presented by Lovelace to
the House on the 30th of April 1642, and for which
he was imprisoned, see C. H. Wilkinson's *Lovelace*
(1925), I, xxiii–xxxvi.

ll. 33–50 According to Wood, *Ath. Ox.* (Bliss, iii,
460), Lovelace was 'much admired and adored by
the female sex'.

Page 156. *Upon the death of Lord Hastings.* Henry,
Lord Hastings, who died of small-pox on the 24th
of June 1649, was the eldest son of Ferdinando,
sixth Earl of Huntingdon. Marvell's verses with those
of seven other poets, five of them *alumni* of Westminster (including Dryden), were added to a volume
called *Lachrymæ Musarum* published in 1649 on the
young nobleman's death as the book was going
through the press. A second issue of the book is
dated 1650.

l. 12 *Remora*] this fish is constantly mentioned in
seventeenth-century poetry. Remoras hung on to
the raft in the Kon-Tiki Expedition.

l. 18 *Geometrick year*] Heavenly justice is weighed in
geometric proportion. Martinius' *Lexicon* (1623).

ll. 43–6 *Hymeneus*] Hastings died when he was about
to be married to the daughter of Sir Theodore
Mayerne, the famous physician. For an analysis of
these lines, see W. Empson's *Seven Types of Ambiguity* (1947 edn.). 'Saffron (l. 44) is merely the
colour of a marriage, purple of a mourning, robe.'

Page 158. *An Elegy upon the Death of My Lord Francis
Villiers.* Lord Francis Villiers was the posthumous

son of George Villiers, first Duke of Buckingham. He was born on the 2nd of April 1629 and was killed near Kingston-on-Thames on the 7th July 1648.

The only known copy of the verses is a quarto of eight pages in the library of Worcester College, Oxford. George Clarke (1660–1730) wrote on it 'by Andrew Marvell'. Clarke was a scholarly collector, and an M.P. who held important positions. He left a collection of books, plays and manuscripts to two Oxford colleges, chiefly to Worcester. Weight must be attached to his ascription as he was much interested in poetry, besides being a man of affairs. His manuscript ascriptions have generally turned out to be correct. Margoliouth reprinted it for the first time; but points out that if it is by Marvell, it is his one unequivocally royalist utterance: he gives no substantial additional evidence for the poem being by Marvell. I include it with reservation, but the poem might well have been written by him. A valuable note on George Clarke by Mr. C. H. Wilkinson written for Margoliouth's edition (I, p. 332) gives all the available reasons for the inclusion of the poem.

Mrs. Duncan Jones has suggested to me that *Clora*, l. 69, may be Mary Kirke, the daughter of A. Townsend.

INDEX OF FIRST LINES

INDEX OF FIRST LINES